THE GAMBINO MAFIA CRIME FAMILY

The Complete History of
New York Crime Organization

Table of Contents

INTRODUCTION

The history of the Mafia is over a century old, but the early days were steeped in mystery and rumors. These underground figures were so far removed from most people's daily lives that they only became part of their world when it was depicted on film or in fiction. Books and films became the stuff of legends regarding gangsters and mob life, while on the streets of New York and other major cities in the USA (and back in Italy), the Mafia was a major organization using extortion and other racketeering activities to fund their operations.

The violent, bloody life of gangsters and mobsters was governed by a particular code of morals and rules, and this seemed to make them more interesting to the public. They were elevated to a higher state of recognition compared to ordinary criminals, and sometimes they were given folk hero titles. Was life so mundane that violent criminals were a chance to bring a sense of excitement to daily life? Remember what life was like back then. Two world wars and the Great Depression formed a society that must have welcomed tales of ordinary men rising from their low beginnings and becoming successful even though they did it through crime.

As society evolved, so did the Mafia, especially the Gambino family. They seemed to have an innate survival instinct that kept them at the fore of the Cosa Nostra and ensured they emerged victorious even through the darkest of times. Their leaders have been the stuff of legends, and they remain a part of the most colorful family in mob lore. Al Capone may have dominated the headlines of the day, but he was neither a "rich man" nor a Sicilian, so he wasn't considered part of the elite, which may explain why he moved from New York to Chicago. Welcome to the world of the Mafia and the Gambino family, the very heart of organized crime.

CHAPTER 1:
The History of The New York Gangs

In the last ten years of the nineteenth century and the first decade of the twentieth century, over two and a half million Italians migrated to America. The prospect of better wages and regular work lured them, and most originated from an area in the south of Italy where half the adult population relied on agricultural jobs, which were poorly paid and offered irregular income, depending on the seasons and the crops. America was the land of milk and honey, and they flocked to fill the need for unskilled labor. They hoped to benefit from the wealth and opportunity that America offered and to become part of this emerging new economy.

Unfortunately, most immigrants knew little of how to travel there and had no contacts who would help them settle into accommodation or find jobs. An enterprising group of Italian men, known by the term *padrones,* formed contract labor systems to help the immigrants. These seemingly helpful padrones would charge the immigrants for their services but promised they would find high-paying jobs and decent accommodation once they landed on American shores.

The new arrivals in America were coached on what they should say to immigration control to ensure they secured a place in the new world, and they were warned to trust nobody except their compatriots. Americans weren't to be trusted, and the immigrants were instructed to stick to their story and only listen to the padrone. Once they arrived, the immigrants were packed into cramped and unsanitary accommodations and told they must travel from city to city to find work.

Life was tough, and the padrones functioned as intermediaries between the fresh arrivals and the employers who needed them. They would secure workers at a low pay rate before renting them out to contractors at a hugely increased rate. Because the Italians often spoke little English and had an inbuilt mistrust of Americans, they were unaware of how the padrones were profiting from their labor. The padrones were responsible for the highly inflated rents and overpriced provisions they supplied. They also functioned as bankers to the emigres and charged them high rates to ensure their money was kept in a safe place.

New York was one of the major hubs for immigrants, and the rents charged were often half an unskilled worker's salary. The areas they settled in were classed as slums, and one of the most notorious was Mulberry Bend in the Five Points area of Lower Manhattan, where Chinatown is now situated. It is intrinsically associated with Italian American history and was a place featured heavily in the history of the New York Gangs.

Understanding what it was like to live in this area is hard to imagine, but the Italians made it as comfortable as possible. Journalists from the era wrote about the lack of division, with unskilled workers living alongside professional and skilled workers. Some families lived in total squalor, with three or four families sharing the same space, while other dwellings were bright and well-kept. It was described as neat and graceful poverty, living alongside one-room dens of squalor in which multiple families lived. The residents told the journalist that a single building contained a thousand souls.

The Mano Nero

Considering the conditions in which the emigres lived, it was almost inevitable that crime would become a way to rise above the poverty and get out of the squalor of the area now known as "Little Italy." Laws had been passed that meant the power of the padrones had waned, but they hadn't disappeared. They remained a huge part of the Italian community as bankers and employment agents. They continued to collaborate with the American contractors, who flourished from the supply of cheap Italian labor.

In 1903, one such contractor, Nicola Cappiello, who resided in Brooklyn, received a letter demanding a thousand dollars. He was told that, if he didn't pay this amount, his house would be dynamited and his family killed. The letter was signed Mano Nera, which translates as the Black Hand, and was decorated with a symbol of a black hand drawn crudely in the corner. This was the first recorded case of this term being used. It would continue to be applied to the period of violence and extortion that dominated the Italian neighborhoods for the next ten years.

How the name originated is debatable, but some historians believe it originated from a play that had toured American theaters the previous year. In the play, the members of a secret society murdered their victims and left a symbolic Black Hand on the bodies of their victims. To create publicity for the production, staff members in theaters the play was booked to visit would receive notes in the post telling them to "Beware the Black Hand," and this caused one office worker to flee the building, thinking she was under threat from an unknown force.

Following the press reports of the Black Hand letter to Cappiello, the cases of threats and extortion letters grew, with the press making the most of the sensational rise in violence and crime in the

Italian districts. They offered varying explanations about who was behind the phenomenon and often referred to the Sicilian Mafia or forces even more heinous. The Italian communities in New York and Chicago were the most targeted groups by the Black Hand threats, but there were reports from other parts of the country. The New York offenses were so shocking compared to other regions they regularly made the press and created headlines so sensational that they attracted the attention of the Italian consulate.

They conducted their own investigation and discovered that only one case from thirty so-called Black Hand offenses was genuine. The allegations were part of a press conspiracy to make Italian immigrants seem violent and out of control.

However, in 1908, the number of genuine cases of the Black Hand had grown to four hundred and twenty-four, resulting in forty-four bomb explosions. Just five years later, this number had risen to one hundred in the first seven months of 1913, and the police were struggling to cope with the caseload. A struggling NYPD had just forty officers who could speak both English and Italian, and only four were fluent in the Sicilian dialect the Black Hand perps favored.

During the twelve years of the Black Hand Society, nobody ever discovered who founded the movement, who conducted the bombings, or who was the mastermind running the operations. They had become part of folklore, and over time, they became part of the organization known as the Mafia, which became an umbrella term for Italian lawbreakers. Some experts believe the Black Hand society was a term used to cover any activities carried out by Italian desperadoes and scattered lawbreakers to give the press a meatier story with more sensational headlines. Any individual found breaking the law only had to announce themselves as a member of the Black Hand for them to be associated with the prestige of an organization reportedly responsible for tens of thousands of individuals.

Meanwhile, the boss of bosses, Guiseppe Morello, saw a way to profit from the notoriety of the Black Hand extortion letters and offered a service to wealthy Italians who received their missives. He acted as an adversary between the gang and their wealthy victims and reportedly made more money as a go-between than if he had written the letters himself. His family doctor offered him free treatment for life if he would guarantee his safety after he received a threatening letter. Yet, rumors appeared that the mob boss was also secretly extorting his own attorney to secure lower legal fees.

Suspicions were raised about Morello's connection to the letters because they were often delivered to the victim when he "just happened to be in the same place at the same time," and he was on hand to register the shock and fear the victim displayed and was quick to offer his help. The victim fully knew the mob leaders' connections and saw a way to escape the tricky situation in which they had found themselves. Morello then told them that the Black Hand would only kill their victims when they had no choice, and they wanted to make a point. He offered to take the letter back, find the man who wrote it, and persuade him to drop the extortion for a fee. The victim gratefully paid, and Morello then left with the letter that was never returned to the victim but with his fee in his pocket. When the victim recovered his wits and realized the mob boss may have duped him, he had no evidence to take to the authorities and no way to prove his claim. Perhaps it was a Black Hand letter, and perhaps it was Morello cashing in on their notoriety, but they would never know.

When the police did raid Morello's homes, they found letters addressed to victims supposedly from the Black Hand society. They were badly written and contained phrases that seemed very "Mafia-like" with references to people of honor, kissing of the forehead under penalty of death that seemed to suggest the writer was Italian. English was their second language.

Although the main group known as the Black Hand Society was never claimed by any individual, some people linked with the crimes became prominent Mafia members. Jack Ignatius Dragna was linked with the Black Hand and became the boss of an LA crime family, dubbed the "Capone of LA" by Mafia members and local law enforcement. Joe Pinzolo was a former Black Hander and went on to lead the New York City crime family known as the Lucchese Family before his death in 1930 during the Cantalamessa War.

The White Hand Society

By 1907, something had to be done to lessen the threats posed by the Black Hand, even though nobody knew who was ultimately responsible for their membership. Three prominent Italian groups banded together and formed the White Hand society that aimed to defeat the Black Hand and remove the threat of extortion. Their efforts were short-lived, and most of their leaders were targeted and faced extortion and death threats. It was decided they needed more firepower, and the police were recruited to make sure a meeting of five hundred Italian volunteers was safe when they met to create a new organization named the Italian Vigilance Protection Association. It formed local subcommittees that would gather intelligence from their communities and give it to the police to aid their inquiries. The police commissioner at the time added his support with a plan to form a secret squad of his top officers to deal with the Black Hand threat, but they were denied funding by the city's finance committee. Undeterred, the head of the squad sought private funding and was named Lt. Joseph Petrosino.

The squad achieved moderate success but was hit by tragedy in 1909 when Petrosino was assassinated in Sicily on a fact-finding mission. The squad was shaken, and when the news was announced, it was revealed the crack squad now contained just four men. New York once more experienced elevated rates of extortion and kidnapping crimes. In 1913 the number of bombings and violence against victims rose to unprecedented levels, and the Black Hand was once again dominating the headlines. Things were changing in Europe and America as the levels of immigration fell, and the new police commissioner of New York brought in stricter laws against extortion, which led to falling crime rates. The Great War dominated the headlines, and the Black Hand threat finally dissipated after a twelve-year reign of terror.

Did the Black Hand exist as an organized crime group? Probably not. Nobody claimed leadership, and only a handful of notorious names were attached to their ranks. The term was more likely used to cover crimes designed to extract money and favors from the wealthy by members of society who had finally had enough of being exploited. The fear and notoriety the name Black Hand conjured would have appealed to Italians who wanted to be part of the Mafia but who didn't have the connections or the influence needed to get noticed.

Sending letters signed with the notorious Black Hand moniker must have seemed like a straightforward way to become part of a powerful group without having to gain their favor or rise through the ranks. For even the lowliest part of society, this must have been a tempting way to get easy money. Did they commit the bombings or other violence attached to the threats? Maybe, maybe not. There was a lot of construction happening in the city, and they would have had access to dynamite and the means to detonate it and could have been behind the bombings.

The fact is we will never know, but the most compelling fact must be the lack of a named leader. Italian mob bosses and their underlings weren't shy about claiming their crimes, and if the Black Hand did have structure and leadership, it would have been claimed. Despite this, there can be no disputing the Black Hand and the twelve years it claimed headlines, especially in New York, formed the forerunners of the crime families that would reign until the present day.

The Main Men in the Gambino Timeline

Ignazia Lupo

One of the most notorious figures in the early history of American gangs was born in Palermo to a middle-class family in 1877. Although his family was respectable, le Ignazio Lupo soon found he had a taste for crime and was regularly involved in petty theft and robbery. At twenty-two, he committed his first murder when he retaliated against a knife attack by a man named Salvatore Morelli and shot him dead. The police soon discovered the gunman's name and filed charges of murder, but Ignazio followed the advice of his family and fled Italy to the shores of England. He landed in Liverpool but set his sights on America and traveled extensively before settling in New York in 1898. Back at home, he was convicted in absentia of the murder of Morelli the following year, which made sure he would never return to his birthplace.

Once he had settled in New York, he joined a cousin and opened a retail store in downtown Manhattan. As the store thrived, his father joined them, and they opened another store and took over a local bar. At 25, Ignazia was a joint owner of two successful retail outlets and a bar, but he still wasn't satisfied. He resorted to the tactics the Black Hand faction used to terrorize the Little Italy community and extort funds.

Throughout his lifetime, Lupo is believed to have been responsible for over sixty murders and his partnership with two mob bosses, called Nicholas Morello and Ciro Terranova. In 1902, a local grocer dared to speak out about Lupo, Morello, and Ciro operating a counterfeiting operation and called for the community to fight back and report the gangsters. The faction didn't take kindly to his interference, and the man known as Joe the Grocer was found with horrendous injuries, including a slit throat from one ear to the other, stuffed into an old potato sack. The Lupo faction sent a clear message to the local community to put up and shut up, or the same could happen to them.

The following year, a series of murders began that shocked even the most hardened criminals and enhanced the reputation of Lupo and his associates even further. In New Orleans, the Provenzano family ruled the Italian district and had committed two murders where they left the body in a barrel for the police to find. The idea must have appealed to the Lupo alliance. Benedetto Madonia, a local stonemason, was a vocal opponent of the crime group. He became the first victim of the gang to be found in a barrel of sawdust with their trademark slit throat and over twenty stab wounds on his body.

Several members of the crime group were brought in for questioning, and some were arrested but later released because of a lack of evidence. They continued to rule the New York streets for the next six years, with even more murders and extortion, until they finally pushed their luck too far in 1910. The police conducted raids on Morello and Lupo's homes and found compelling evidence of counterfeiting and extortion. The pair were arrested alongside a group of associates, and their trial began two weeks later. The jury took a mere hour and 15 minutes to decide their fate. Morello and Lupo were both found guilty and sentenced to 15 years of jail time and a fine of $500.

Lupo served his sentence in the US penitentiary in Atlanta, where he proved to be far from the model prisoner. Throughout his sentence, he was in and out of solitary and consistently on a restricted diet as punishment for his unruly behavior. This included spitting at the correctional officers and trying to bribe the staff to send out letters. These petty crimes were superseded when inmates murdered the Deputy Warden of the prison thought to be on Lupo's payroll. Although he denied any knowledge of the assassination, some inmates described him as "being just six feet" from the murder, where he could witness and enjoy the brutal killing.

Although the evidence pointed to his involvement, no charges were filed, and Lupo was eventually released from prison in 1920 after his sentence was changed to include time served. Following his release, Lupo returned to Italy but yearned for his American home. When he returned, he was initially stopped at immigration but convinced them he was a wine importer and would be a model citizen. Although he rejoined the Mafia and sought to rise through the ranks, he was a shadow of his former self. The newly created commission decided his reputation as a murderer brought too much attention to the organization. Hence, they attempted to silence him by stripping him of his rank and leaving him a solitary lottery operation to run.

Lupo wasn't happy, and to regain his former Mafia position, he extorted local bakeries and convinced them to join his new union, a crude way of labeling his protection racket. When one baker refused to conform, Lupo brutally murdered him and once more attracted the attention of the law. In 1935, he was deemed a public menace by President Franklin Roosevelt. He was sent back to prison for breaking the conditions of his release and returned to Atlanta penitentiary. The local press described his arrival as the return of the "oldest living public enemy in the United States" and described his appearance as "a grizzled terrorist formerly known as Lupo the Wolf." He served an additional ten years and was released in 1946, shortly before his death in 1947, when he died without ceremony as a virtual unknown.

However, Lupo made an important connection with the "first boss of the Gambino family" through his association with Morello. Salvatore "Toto" D'Aquila was the main man behind the organized crime that came from Sicily and took root in New York in the early part of the 20th century. He was an old-school criminal referred to as a "mustache Pete" type of criminal who arrived in America having committed their first murders back in Italy.

The younger Sicilians who landed in America fresh off the boat were labeled the Young Turks. Still, they recognized that older, established members of the criminal fraternity were important contacts. D'Aquila and some of these younger Sicilians banded together to form a cheese importing business to mask his underworld activities. He aligned himself with another mustache Pete Morello and worked alongside him as his trusted aide and confidante. He was arrested twice in the early 1900s, but all charges were dropped, indicating the influence of Morello. Following Morello's imprisonment in 1910 alongside Lupo, it was reported that D'Aquila took charge of the Morello gang, but he faced competition from another source. Joe Masseria was a former capo of Morello and felt he was better qualified to take over the gang's leadership.

Knowing when he was beaten, D'Aquila moved from the Morello crew and formed his own gang in East Harlem and the Bronx, with loyal members of the Morello gang joining him and becoming his trusted aides. D'Aquila also recognized this was the time for a change, instigating the first attempt to unite the separate families into an organized unit and bring order to the separate factions. His efforts were met with derision, and his attempt to become the big boss of the Italian gangs failed, but he was left with plenty of financially successful operations.

When Morello was released from prison in 1920, he found the Morello gang was struggling and lacking power. D'Aquila hatched a plot to remove Morello and his top associates and tasked his top associate, Umberto Valenti, with the task. Then followed a two-year period when Valenti conducted several attempts to kill Morello and his partner Masseria. Although he took out a couple of cousins and bodyguards, the main targets continued to evade him. In 1922, Valenti attended a meeting with the heads of the warring factions to settle the dispute, but he was the only person to turn up. As he waited for the others, he realized it was a trap and turned to flee as Lucky Luciano and several gunmen appeared and shot him dead as he attempted to get into a taxi.

With his main ally dead, D'Aquila felt the shift of power, and he failed to stop his allies from defecting to the Masseria and Morello gang. Although he was respected, he became the subject of an assassination plot in which a former underboss named Al Mineo was promised the leadership of the D'Aquila gang if he took out the head of the organization. D'Aquila left his home for a medical appointment on the 10th of October 1928 and was gunned down. Subsequently, Mineo took over the organization that eventually became the Gambino crime family.

CHAPTER 2:

The Emergence of the New York Gangs, the Rise of the Sicilians

As America and the rest of the world was reeling from the effects of the Great War from 1914 to 1918 and the unprecedented loss of life, servicemen returned home to a country that held little promise. There had been an anti-temperance society movement for decades in America, and prohibition of the sale and consumption of alcohol gained further support from the Suffragette movement and the evangelical congregations. They believed alcohol was the main reason family life and society were affected by drunkenness. Industrialists of the time also welcomed the temperance movement, believing it would increase the effectiveness of their workforce.

In 1917, as the war still raged in Europe, the U.S. Congress passed the Eighteenth Amendment, which illegalized the production, transportation, and sale of alcohol. Two years later, they further amended the act to include over three-quarters of the country and introduced it into the constitution. The same year, the Volstead Act passed, which made Prohibition nationwide, and the moratorium on all alcohol-related business stayed in place for the next thirteen years.

Bootlegging and Gangsterism

Although the Eighteenth Amendment and the following Volstead Act was intended to make society better and increase productivity, they were doomed to fail from the day they began. The enforcement agencies formed to stamp down on illegal economies, named bootlegging and speakeasies by the people who ran them, were ineffectual and often prone to corruption. Distilling options from across the border provided early bootleggers with perfect opportunities to bring foreign liquor to American outlets.

The Italian gangs that had formerly concentrated on extortion and other forms of crime to fill their coffers saw multiple ways to expand their businesses with illegal liquor sales. Early bootleggers made connections in the Bahamas, Mexico, and Canada to supply them with hooch to sell to illegal drinking dens. The problems increased when these rumrunners realized there was a point of entry just five kilometers outside of Atlantic City that was beyond the authority of the US Government.

The bootleggers used vessels registered in other countries to transport liquor to this landing point and then loaded the contents onto high-powered crafts created especially to outrun the coast guard ships assigned to the area. During the first few years of Prohibition, the distribution of illegal alcohol and the capture of bootleggers underwent many stages. The coast guard became more successful by building faster crafts and widening the area where they stopped boats. The bootleggers found a stash of alcohol rendered undrinkable by adding toxic chemicals. They employed top chemists to help "wash" the toxic chemicals from the alcohol and sell them to illegal drinking dens.

Bootleggers used illegal stills and other outlets to manufacture their own brands of spurious alcohol and corn-based spirits to distribute to the public. The people responsible for this distribution of alcohol and the opening of popular speakeasies meant Prohibition didn't stop the country from drinking. Still, in the late 1920s and early 1930s, it cemented the importance of organized crime. It led to the Italian bootleggers and the Mafia crime syndicates forming what became the New York Gang synonymized with the term organized crime group.

There was a thriving Mafia presence in Chicago, with Al Capone, Big Jim Colosimo, and Johnny Torrio all gaining notoriety and wealth. They were joined by Lucky Luciano, Bugsy Seigel, and other notable gangsters, and in 1927, Capone's wealth was estimated at over $100 million.

The New York Gangs

Back in the Big Apple, a gangster named Salvatore Maranzano was gaining a reputation as a gangster with influence. He wasn't your typical mob boss. He was a mediator for the other gangs and a calming influence for the Italian American factions, but he had his detractors.

Salvatore Maranzano

His early life was in the Sicilian town of Castellammare del Golfo, where he was raised in a God-fearing household, and he initially went to a religious school to train to join the priesthood. Another path beckoned, and he soon became involved in the Mafia activities rife in the area. He married a local woman, called Elizabetta, who happened to be the daughter of a prominent mob boss, and soon rose through the ranks of the organization.

Maranzano wasn't your typical thug. He was intelligent and erudite, and he proved himself loyal to the boss of the Sicilian mob family Don Vito Cascio Ferro, who decided the promising young mobster should immigrate to the States and become the face of the Sicilian faction. He arrived in the US in 1919 as a real estate broker but soon dropped that facade and moved into the rackets most associated with mobsters. Alcohol, extortion, prostitution, and protection gave him the perfect opportunities to become a well-known name in New York.

When Prohibition became law, Maranzano set up a large distillery in a nearby suburb and became a major part of the gang known as the Castellammare. A rival group, led by Joe Masseria, was looking to halt the growth of the gang by demanding payments from the Castellammare leaders. At first, the Don of the gang, Cola Schiro, paid and continued with the alcohol distilling. Under pressure to fight back, Schiro eventually went into hiding, and the gang was taken over by Vito Bonventre, with Maranzano taking a higher role in the group.

The Castellammare was ready for battle, but let's look at the main players they recruited to bring help when they went to war against Masseria and his troops.

Gaspar Milazzo

Once a high-level mobster in Brooklyn, Milazzo was a highly respected Sicilian member of the Mafia. He maintained his connections after moving to Detroit and joining the Sicilian population and the gang named the Jewish Purple Gang that ran a successful bootlegging operation. He was a leading light in the underground Sicilian/Italian underworld and respected for his sense of fairness and mediation.

He created a close working relationship with another Detroit Mafia leader, and together they created a cohesive criminal unit that contained some of the most influential Mafia members in the area. They controlled bootlegging, prostitution, and their illegal rackets with extraordinarily little trouble between the factions. They gained a reputation for stopping the bloody battles and conflicts of the previous decade. They formed a united front that offered their forces to the Castellammare gang whenever needed. The Detroit Mafia Godfather was a powerful ally, and he was ready to join the war.

Joe Aiello

While Al Capone may have been the face of Chicago, he wasn't Sicilian and, as such, felt less kinship with Maranzano. When the Castellammare boss sought help from Chicago mobsters, he turned to a fellow Sicilian, Aiello, who had lived and worked in New York before he left in 1920 to head west to Chicago, where he eventually headed the Sicilian underworld movement, much to the annoyance of Capone.

During Prohibition, he controlled most of the criminal elements in an area known as Little Sicily, so he controlled a vast majority of the city's speakeasies and drinking dens. Capone refused to let him have his territory and continued to meddle in his business, which angered other high-ranking Mafia officials, who recognized Aiello was trying to control his territories. The conflict came to a head in 1929, and when he tried to mediate, Masseria from New York not only failed to resolve the issues, but he also offended Aiello so badly that, when Maranzano asked for his help against Masseria, Aiello quickly agreed to send his men to fight alongside him.

While his men were fighting in the Castellammarese conflict, Capone saw his chance and sent his troops to assassinate Aiello on the corner of Kolmar Avenue. Aiello was waiting for a taxi when Capone's gunmen saw their chance and killed him in October 1930.

Stefano Magaddino

When you read historical reports of Mafia organizations, you think of big cities and sometimes an honorable mention of Miami. Still, an overlooked part of Mafia history was taking part in Buffalo, whose location meant the bootleggers of the Buffalo Crime Family had easy access to Canadian sources of alcohol.

Stefano Magaddino was born in Castellammare Del Golfo in 1891 and immigrated to America at the age of ten. He and his family lived in Brooklyn, where he went to school but was soon distracted by the New York Mafia activities, which is unsurprising given their lucrative opportunities. He found a kinship in the organization that welcomed him, and soon, he gained a reputation for enforcement. Magaddino's brother was killed during a dispute with another prominent New York gang. Stefano allegedly killed the man who shot him, forcing him to flee the area to avoid arrest. He settled in Buffalo and built the phenomenally successful Crime Family into a prosperous and empiric association.

His initial cover for his criminal activities was a successful funeral business that led to his Mafia nickname "The Undertaker" rather than any other more bloodthirsty reasons. Magaddino remained a shadowy figure in the organization and shunned the limelight, unlike some of his Mafia counterparts, and he concentrated on running a successful business. The organization obtained wine and spirits from Canada, which they then distributed to downtown New York and beyond. His contacts included some of the most important mobsters in the country, including Maranzano, and their shared birthplace ensured his support in the war against Masseria.

Magaddino was one of the longest-serving mob bosses and ran an extraordinarily successful illicit business, as well as numerous legitimate concerns. He reportedly extended his territory to include the Old World, including Asia, Europe, and other territories. He was part of the infamous Mafia Commission and served time as its Don. He remained in a position of power in Buffalo until the late 1960s, when his son's home was raided, and copious amounts of cash were found hidden in suitcases.

The rest of the Buffalo Crime Family were angry and saw the cash as the illicit gains siphoned off what should have been the gang's money, and they rebelled against the elderly boss and ousted him from leadership. The year after the rebellion, Magaddino suffered a serious heart attack and died in his home. He was interred at his favorite place, Niagara Falls, where his grave remains to this day.

A small footnote about Magaddino: he may not have been the most well-known mobster of the era, but he should be remembered for his foresight and innovation. He created one of the most lucrative empires in an area severely underdeveloped and considered a backwater in American terms. He served as a Mafia Don for longer than any other individual, and he took his business beyond the borders that restricted other racketeers. He should be remembered with the respect he deserves and not consigned to the wastebasket of history.

Salvatore Sabella

Another famous son of Castellammare del Golfo Sabella was born in 1891 and enrolled as a butcher's apprentice in the town at fourteen. The young apprentice killed the butcher when he was subjected to his violent outbursts. He was sentenced to three years in jail in Milan, where he made important connections and honed his criminal skills. Upon his release, he immediately joined the Sicilian Mafia. He was sponsored to immigrate to America in 1912 to join D'Aquila and other immigrants from the area to form a successful organization.

Seven years later, Sabella had shown such promise he was sent to Philadelphia to form a branch of the organization and train future mob bosses. A couple of the recruits decided they would rather give orders than take them, and they organized an uprising that was promptly reported to Sabella. The two dissidents were shot and killed on a street corner, and this put Sabella in the frame for their murders. Although he was acquitted of the crime, the authorities discovered his illegal citizenship and deported him back to Sicily in 1927.

As he watched the news and saw the reports of the infamous Castellammarese war raging, he felt he had to return to New York and lend his support to his compatriot Maranzano. He recruited nine gunmen to join him in the fight against Masseria. Following the end of the war, he returned to Philadelphia to run his former gang, but he seemed to have lost his edge. At forty, following the bloody battles of the Castellammarese war, he decided he was too old for all the violence and feared for his own safety. He was arrested for assault that year, and although he was acquitted, he retired from organized crime and moved to Norristown in Pennsylvania. In this quiet but populous area, he worked as a butcher until his death from natural causes in 1962.

Sabella was one of the lucky ones, who managed to leave behind his nefarious beginnings and have a "normal" life, although the irony of his final choice of profession is amusing, considering the crime he committed at fourteen.

The Castellammarese War

While tensions bubbled and the era of the Mustache Pete-type gangsters was in decline, it was time for resolutions. Masseria and Maranzano may both have been born in the same region, but they didn't believe in sharing the power they held. The Mafia was in disarray, with the two leaders fighting over territory and risking leadership challenges from the young Turks rising through the ranks and challenging them to change their old-fashioned ways and work with non-Italians to create more opportunities.

The hostilities began in 1930, with Masseria ordering a hit on one of Maranzano's top allies, Gaspar Milazzo. Still, the young gunman from Genoa failed to get his original target. Instead, he killed another member of the gang, named Reina, who was part of an important family based in New York, which led to them switching alliances and joining Maranzano and his men. Following Reina's murder, the Masseria troops suffered several blows with two murders of prominent members of the gang.

However, the Masseria gang wasn't beaten yet. They retaliated by taking out Joe Aiello on the streets of Chicago. This seemed to be one killing too far for the Masseria troops, and they defected to the Castellammare faction, making Maranzano the more powerful force. The two main Masseria allies negotiated with Maranzano and gave them his support, providing he stopped the war and brought peace back to the streets of New York. A plan was hatched, where Lucky Luciano would continue to show support to Masseria to get him to a certain destination where a group of gunmen, including Bugsy Siegel and Joe Adonis, were waiting for him. The story goes that, during a game of cards at the Villa, Tammaro in Brooklyn Luciano excused himself to go to the bathroom, and four shooters burst into the room and gunned down Masseria in cold blood.

The getaway driver was so shaken up by their actions he failed to start the car and had to be shoved out of the way by Siegel, who ensured the group made a clean getaway. The police report stated

Masseria was seated at a table with two or three unknown men when he was killed by several men who shot him in the head, back, and chest area. His autopsy showed Masseria hadn't eaten and had died with an empty stomach, a fact that indicated the level of contempt he had nurtured from his former allies.

The Five Families

After Masseria's death, Maranzano ended the war and restructured the Mafia in New York City. He allotted the areas of the city to five families headed by a boss with a structured series of underbosses and other ranks responsible for crews of soldiers and associates in line to become members.

The five families were named:

1. The Masseria family, who would become the Genovese family led by Lucky Luciano.

2. The Profaci family, who would become the Colombo family, led by Joseph Profaci.

3. The Reina family, who would become the Lucchese family led by Thomas Gagliano.

4. The Castellammare family, who would become the Bonanno family, led by Maranzano.

5. The D'Aquila/ Mineo family, who would become the Gambino family, led by Frank Scalice.

Although the five families were considered equally important, Maranzano immediately assembled the other bosses at a village in Dutchess County, New York, where he declared himself the capo di tutti capi, or the boss of all bosses, which didn't sit well with Luciano and some of the other young Turks in the organization.

The family groups were organized in a pyramid structure, where the head of the family was the boss and was responsible for all sections of his organization.

- The Boss
- The Underboss The consigliere
- Caporegime
- Soldiers
- Associates

While the structure of the Mafia was supposed to stop the abuse of power in the New York area, Maranzano wasn't as fair as he professed to be. The gain of power led to his eventual downfall, as the other family leaders witnessed him pocketing the profits from their districts rather than distributing them among the whole organization. As his abuse grew and angered the other leaders, so did the list of people wanting to put a bullet in his head.

Maranzano's Death

Just six months after the war had finished and he had taken control of the New York Mafia, a hit was called on Maranzano by Lucky Luciano by an up-and-coming associate, named Meyer Lansky, who was one of the first non-Italians to rise through the ranks, having been born in Russia. On the 10th of September 1931, five gunmen dressed as police officers entered Maranzano's office and stabbed and shot him dead. The hitmen was aided by a trusted Maranzano soldier, who was tasked with pointing out Maranzano to them, as they didn't know what he looked like.

Interesting fact: The only pictures of Maranzano on record are the crime scene pictures of his death. There was reported to be a headshot found in police records, but that was soon proved to be false. Maranzano was a highly private man compared to his Mafia counterparts, who loved photo opportunities.

The shooters fled the scene and encountered another mobster, called Vincent Coll, who was attending a meeting with Maranzano to organize a hit on Luciano and the top members of his gang. Coll raced from the building and avoided both the police officers and the hitmen, who were thought to have included Bugsy Seigel and a young Turk named Bo Weinberg, who would later be known as Dutch Schultz.

CHAPTER 3:
The Formation of the Cosa Nostra

S o, the war was over, and Maranzano was deposed, with Lucky Luciano now taking the reins. He was savvy enough to know where Maranzano had failed as the Boss and why he had been taken out, so he resolved to make significant changes in 1931. Although the term Cosa Nostra wouldn't become part of common parlance until decades later, he formed the Commission, which meant the original five families would create a CEO position. This leader would be part of a board of commissioners that made decisions collectively. He scrapped the title of the capo di tutti and created a conglomerate of representatives that all had a say in the decisions surrounding the Mafia business.

It was decided the Italian Mafia and the Cosa Nostra, whose name meant "Our thing," wouldn't be combined to make one organization, but the two factions would run alongside each other. The older Italian Mafia ways would remain with more traditional ways and keep their heritage alive. At the same time, the new Cosa Nostra would make way for the new ideas brought by Luciano and his contemporaries. There followed a written code of morals, pledges, and rules to follow, and becoming part of the Cosa Nostra was no easy job.

The Initiation Ceremony

Becoming a fully-fledged member of the Cosa Nostra was known as "being made," and certain criteria had to be fulfilled. When someone applied to become a recruit, they were told the rules and pledges to which they would have to adhere. The Cosa Nostra was a family for life and must come before any other part of the recruit's life, and they must be on call every hour of every day (the phrase 24/7 hadn't been coined then.) The family was their main concern, and they must accept any jobs they were given, from the most mundane tasks to the more serious ones higher up the scale.

The Code of Omerta

They would be informed that the Code of Omerta should be their mantra if the authorities questioned them. The law originated in Sicily and was translated as "manhood," which referred to the ability of real men to solve their own problems with no help from any organization representing the law. For instance, if a gangster attacked another gangster, the victim would never name his attacker, no matter how much bad blood flowed between them.

The rule originated from early Sicilians, who were subject to a Spanish regime in the 16th century. They felt so oppressed and humiliated by the ruling party they took a vow to stick together and fight their overlords with a strict code of silence and deal with their personal grievances in-house. The stain of being labeled an informant was so destructive it was seen as the most heinous act possible. Men should deal with their grievances like men and never resort to government or law agencies to settle them.

The shame of blabbing to the authorities was so great it meant their soul would burn in hell. In the initiation stage of becoming "made," the head of the family would light a playing card with a saint's face on it and place it on their hand while they pricked the finger with a pin to make it bleed. These were symbols of the oath and their commitment to the Cosa Nostra. It would be explained that, if they broke the commandments or the Code of Omerta, they would burn in hell just like the saint was burning on their hand and that their blood represented the allegiance bound in blood. Break that allegiance, and their blood would be shed.

The Rules of the Cosa Nostra

Also called the commandments, breaking these rules was punishable by death, which was set in stone. Below is a general description of these rules, which were worded differently depending on the ruling family, but all meant the same thing.

Who couldn't become part of the Costa Nostra:

- People who had family ties with law enforcement
- Anyone with sentimental betrayals in the family

If anyone in your family had shown the wrong types of behavior and you supported them, you would be barred from admission to the Cosa Nostra. For instance, if your brother cheated on his wife with his friend's wife and you let him stay with you, it would be frowned upon. You needed to comply with the moral code even through association.

- People who were badly behaved and had no morals

While this may seem strange, the Mafia and the Cosa Nostra were very moral organizations. The only difference was the set of morals to which they adhered.

The Morals of the Cosa Nostra

1. A third party must be involved if one party wishes to make an association with another. This was a simple show of respect and meant, when you approached a powerful person or group, you went through the correct channels and never presumed you were important enough to contact them directly. To become a man of many friends, you need to know how to conduct yourself.

2. Never look at the wives of friends. Even if they throw themselves at you or promise you the earth with a guaranteed lack of comeback, you should never betray your brothers. The main rule was to keep it in your pants unless it's a girl in Vegas or you have no connection to the girl's fellow. If you do betray your friend or brother in this way, then expect the worst. You have been dishonorable, and the wounded party will decide your fate.

3. Never be seen associating with the law. Even if your best childhood friend joins the force, from that day on, they are dead to you. This rule is all about snitching and how the Cosa Nostra hates anyone who tells tales. Don't be that guy; sort your troubles like a man.

4. Don't go to clubs for fun. The Cosa Nostra expected its members to have had their fun in their younger days and expected that, by their thirties, their members should be family men who use pubs and clubs solely for meetings and business matters. You should be following your life path, not partying like a madman.

5. Nothing supersedes the Cosa Nostra's business. Even if your wife is about to give birth or your mother is on her deathbed, you must answer the call when needed. Of course, family comes first, but the Cosa Nostra considers themselves your ultimate family while your regular family takes second place.

6. Respect wives and mothers. This was one of the biggest downfalls of gangsters; they treated women as second-class citizens. Women who are associated with the Mafia and the Cosa Nostra are high-quality women with an innate sense of who is a real man. Try to play mind games with these ladies, and they will show you up as a little boy. Be a whole package

with the ladies, and get them to fall for you and be the partner you deserve.

7. Be respectful. If you give your word or make an appointment, then do what you should; arrive at the time and place with respect for the other party. Breaking your word is a sign of a weak personality and shows you have no respect for others or yourself. Be a man of your word.

8. Tell the truth. This may seem like a strange one, but it fits the rest of the commandments. If you lie, it is a sign of fear, and telling the truth is cathartic and shows you are a bigger man than other people who resort to lies. If another member asks you something, then being truthful will gain their respect. When the law or the police ask you something, don't lie; just say you know nothing, which is the truth as far as the Code of Omerta dictates.

9. Don't steal. Simple rule: take care of your finances and earn money rather than take it from others.

10. Don't become involved with activities not worthy of the Cosa Nostra. Over the decades, this has changed depending on the ruling committee. Crimes involving children and the elderly have always been against their strict codes, and anybody found participating in these crimes would have been brought to justice. Narcotics and drug involvement depend on the leadership and the era.

The Cosa Nostra founded the notion that even men with the humblest beginnings deserve the chance to become a "Man of Honor" and be responsible for their own destiny. Organized crime gave them the chance to become part of the family the Cosa Nostra relied on, but they must know the consequences. There was no changing your mind or leaving on good terms. This was for life.

CHAPTER 4:
The Mangano Era

O fficially the first Boss of the Gambino crime family, more sharp-eyed readers will have noticed that Frank Scalice was the original head of the Gambino family. Still, Luciano soon realized he wasn't up to the job and needed to be replaced. He chose a man called Vincenzo Giovanni, who had anglicized his name and became Vincent on his passport application in 1911. It was believed he traveled to America to join his mother, Serafina, and had $1,000 when he arrived in the country. His passport was stamped "Non-Immigrant Alien," and he was listed as an American.

In 1912, he met and married Carolina Cusimano, and the couple became the proud parents of four children born before 1919. In June 1920, he traveled through Europe following his naturalization as an American citizen and passed through France and Switzerland before arriving in Italy to settle his estate there. He returned to America with future Mafia boss Jow Profaci and formed his most lucrative business running the Brooklyn waterfront.

As with most Mafia associates, he used a cover of legitimacy to mask his criminal activities. He was listed as an importer and then a real estate agent, but these were just a front. There are very few pictures from the time of Mangano, but some descriptions help paint a picture of this powerful man. He was short, around 5'6", and had an oval face, a ruddy complexion, black hair, and brown eyes. Reports also state he was a physically powerful man, who was known as good company among his compatriots.

Mangano's movements in the 1920s are sketchy, and he stayed under the radar. Still, it was believed his brother Philip and Vincent formed impressive ties with the Mafia and were considered friends with D'Aquila and Scalise in the early part of the decade. They appeared to be associated with the men who organized the killing of D'Aquila, but this is complete speculation. The fact that Mangano was even linked with these underground figures is a strong indication of just how powerful his ties were.

Following the death of Maranzano, the appointment of Frank Scalise as head of the Gambino family lasted around five months. Why he was demoted is a mystery, but speculation suggests Mangano had earned his place by being a survivor and not angering Luciano during the war. Scalise had ticked off Luciano and his cohorts with his defections and changing sides during the conflict, while Mangano remained neutral and loyal. This was a remarkable feat of achievement in a violent and messy time of war, where bodies littered the streets, and the young Turks seemed to set themselves up to rule.

Mangano was the perfect mix of old-fashioned Mustache Pete morals and young Turk ideals. Everyone liked him and considered him a forward thinker, who could rule with respect and power without using fear to control his men. At forty-three, it must have been a momentous moment for Mangano to be named a key player at the table of the modern Cosa Nostra. He had a bright future, and Luciano made sure he was in the right position to make the most of his power. Mangano was also Sicilian and came with that extra seal of approval that made his position even more secure.

The one fly in the ointment was the appointment of Mangano's underboss, Albert Anastasia, another waterfront guy with an impressive pedigree and a polar opposite style of working to

Mangano. Anastasia was a sweat and grime guy, who loved to get down to the piers and mix with the men who buttered his bread. Mangano was more aloof and presented himself as a rich man with clean fingernails, who loved to entertain his crew with home-cooked meals. What was his signature dish? Of course, the Gambino fortune was founded on fish, the piers, and the waterfront, so Vincent had only to click his fingers, and he had access to the best fresh fish in New York.

At first, the two men worked together well. Anastasia had no aspirations to attain the top job and considered Mangano a character who ran a tight ship even if he wasn't the type of man Anastasia would call a friend. On the other hand, Mangano wasn't overly keen on his underboss but recognized Luciano favored him, so he grudgingly worked with him. As the relationship grew, it was well-documented that, physically, the pair often clashed, and their meetings often descended into shoving and pushing sessions that ended in a fistfight at least once.

They were both hotheads, who relied on their physical appearance to intimidate their opponents, and they both had a similar nickname. Mangano was known as "The Executioner," while the younger man Anastasia was the "Lord High Executioner," which suggested Anastasia was more hotheaded.

Let's study the evidence: Made men were never supposed to raise a hand to each other, although it was well-known that they did. However, to raise a hand to a family boss and suffer no consequences was unheard of. In fact, it was a wild and direct violation of one of the Cosa Nostra commandments, which would have ended with a death sentence for anyone else. Still, because of Anastasia's connections and reputation, he seemed untouchable. This must have made Mangano nervous. How did he deal with a man who seemingly could do whatever he liked because he was a known favorite of Luciano?

However, in the 1930s, with the growth of the Gambino family on the waterfront rackets, Mangano worked closely with the International Longshoreman Association and the bosses that controlled the Eastern seaboard and the flow of goods into the ports. Mangano and Anastasia worked together to form the City Democratic Club, which was responsible for a form of democracy favored by their more lethal brothers Philip and Anthony, known as Tough Tony. This club would later be called Murder Inc. and would become part of the more violent history of the Cosa Nostra.

Murder Inc.

Mangano was eventually squeezed out of the Murder Inc. association, and Louis "Lepke" Buchalter took his place to control the Jewish faction of the organization. Albert Anastasia was the man responsible for the Italian faction, and together they ran the ruthless group of hitmen and contract killers who were an arm of Lucky Luciano's more expansive NCS, or National Crime Syndicate.

The Cosa Nostra loved to have titles for the different branches of their operations, and although Luciano ostensibly controlled Murder Inc, the two main men, Anastasia and Buchalter, were given free rein to operate their deadly crew. To outsiders, the setup must have seemed strange. Although the Italian and Jewish factions had different hitmen working for them, the two groups would meet regularly at the Midnight Rose Candy Store in downtown Brooklyn to discuss the orders handed down from the NCS. Most hits were on obscure targets, although some high-profile murders did happen, and the organization is believed to have been responsible for over a thousand deaths in the decade it operated.

The hitmen would be given a weekly retainer to attend the meetings, and there was never a shortage of takers for jobs. The shooters would organize a shift system to cover all hours of the day and night, and the Candy Store was always filled with hitmen waiting for a job.

Hitmen of Murder Inc.

Kid Twist Reles

The spiritual leader of the Jewish faction, Reles, was a go-to hitman for Buchalter. It is reported that he had a hand in over eighty contract killings with the agency. Before he became a lead member of Murder Inc, he fought well for the Mafia. He had killed a powerful group of men known as the Shapiro brothers, who ran the Brownsville Boys gang, and as a result, he was named the new Boss. He and his partner, Bugsy Goldstein, had taken a couple of hits in the war, but they emerged as victors with a reputation for violence.

He would display his penchant for gruesomeness by using an ice pick on his victims and extreme torture methods to extract information. His victims would often be buried alive, so he could listen to their tortured screams as he walked away from their graves. Reles was an intermediate between the bosses and the men on the ground and was considered a valuable asset in the association. He later turned on the Cosa Nostra and turned witnesses against some of his partners to save his own life when implicated in a murder case. More about this in the next chapter!

Harry "Pittsburgh Phil" Strauss

A former member of the Brownsville Boys, Strauss was a tall and handsome figure, who split his time between the candy store and dating women. He even dated the actress Jean Harlot for a while. He was a dedicated killer from an early age, and one of his trademark moves was to tie the victim's legs behind their heads, so they choked to death.

Reles and Bugsy Goldstein looked like gangsters, but Strauss was different. He was a striking figure as he lounged at the candy store, waiting for the next kill and the fee that accompanied it, but his enthusiasm was genuine. Once he completed a kill, he obtained an early copy of the next day's newspaper and then left town for a couple of days. He enjoyed perusing the headlines and reading about his successful kills while relaxing.

Mendy Weiss

Weiss was a long-time associate of Buchalter and joined him as a trusted underling at Murder Inc. Mendy was associated with one of the most notorious hits carried out by the association on Dutch Schultz in 1935. Schultz was convinced the present Federal prosecutor Dewey needed to be disposed of despite being told to back down by the mob bosses. His persistence led to him being gunned down on the street alongside three other men by Weiss and an accomplice. Weiss was a gunman named by Reles and will appear in that account later.

Louis Capone

No relation to the Chicago mobster Al Capone, Louis was an elder statesman of Murder Inc. He ran a successful pastry business when he wasn't on shift with the association and was impressively connected with gangsters from other regions. Capone was another gunman named Rele.

Happy and the Dasher

This pair of hitmen ran the Italian faction of Murder Inc. in a neighborhood known as Ocen Hill. The nickname "happy" was an ironic nod at the true nature of Harry Malone, who was a vicious, snarling bear of a man. He was unpredictable, and his temper was the stuff of legends. His partner was Frank "Dasher" Abbandano, and the pair became the deadliest team the mob had ever known, called "The Combination." One of their most vicious methods was to use an ice pick on their victims before killing them off with a meat cleaver.

They were eventually convicted of the murder of Whitey Rudnick and sentenced to death. They met their fate at the hands of Ol' Sparky in Sing prison in 1942. Both men were executed on the 19th of February.

Charles "The Bug" Workman

Another hitman involved in killing Dutch Schultz fell out with Weiss when he accused him of returning to the body of Schultz to rob the corpse and then wasting time before the police officers arrived. Workman wanted his former associate to face the death sentence for his behavior, but Anastasia and Buchalter refused to hear his pleas. Although the rift was clear, the two hitmen worked together until the demise of Murder Inc., and Workman was one of the two members who walked away with their lives.

After Murder Inc, the Murder of Puggy Feinstein

As Anastasia ran Murder Inc., he also remained Mangano's underboss, and the two managed to put up with the situation and get on with the job. There was a real tradition in the Gambino family, where Lucky and his compatriots would visit the home of Mangano and eat homemade meals. At the same time, they consumed copious amounts of alcohol. He continued to control the gambling action and was known as the Boss, even though Anastasia was the favored man in the family.

In Brooklyn, a failed boxer with a flat nose, called Puggy Feinstein, was spiraling after the breakdown of a relationship and was organizing lavish parties with plenty of gambling opportunities. This former smash-and-grab guy, who had sailed below the radar of the Cosa Nostra, was suddenly attracting the wrong sort of attention. He didn't just organize gambling parties. He devolved into a gambler himself, and suddenly his debts mounted, and he owed money to some important neighborhood characters.

In 1939, the disrespect shown to Mangano and his family was so extreme he approached the Murder Inc. board with an envelope with Feinstein's name in it and told Anastasia, "Al, he's gotta go." It turned out that Mangano had former beef with Feinstein, which meant he pushed for the death sentence, and the execution would later be the reason Mangano earned the nickname "The Executioner."

Feinstein was lured to the home of future mob rat Rele in Brooklyn, where he found two of the most vicious contract killers in Murder Inc.'s books, Straus and Goldstein, waiting for him. As they took the icepick to his face, Feinstein fought back and caused serious damage to a couple of Strauss's fingers. Irate because their victim had injured them, the pair made his death more protracted and painful by looping a rope around his neck that was also attached to his feet, which meant the more he struggled, the more he strangled himself.

The two hitmen watched the hapless victim slowly strangle himself before they took the body to a vacant lot and set fire to it. The police described the murder as one of the most horrific and gruesome they had encountered, even by Murder Inc. standards. When Rele turned state's evidence, he recounted the murder and who had commissioned it, which ultimately meant the hitmen and Mangano were implicated. Still, Vincent avoided prosecution and remained as head of the family. Following the Feinstein murder and the prosecution of the hitmen, Mangano became more insulated and avoided being involved in any serious crime.

As the 1940s approached and the world faced yet another world war, the Cosa Nostra flourished, and Luciano took advantage of the need for goods and supplies. His war efforts have been highly documented, but few accounts mention he would have had to make sure the Mangano family and their control of the docks were on board. They worked side by side, but because Mangano favored less publicity, he rarely took credit for the creation of the alliance between the newer American factions of the Cosa Nostra and the original Italian families.

Following the war, there was significant need for change within the operation, and Lucky Luciano organized a meeting between the bosses of the top factions within the Cosa Nostra at the Hotel Nacional in Cuba. The agenda for the meeting contained significant topics, including what to do about Bugsy Seigel in LA, who was withholding a great deal of money during the construction of the mob-run Flamingo casino. Another item on the agenda was the meteoric rise of the narcotic trade, which had gone global and was responsible for a huge chunk of the mob's income. Lucky wanted to reintroduce the title and position of "Boss of Bosses" to cement his position as the head of the Cosa Nostra.

The meeting went well, and all had a good time, with a stunning performance by Frank Sinatra, a mob favorite, and additional festivities. The bosses agreed the organization needed to adapt to more modern ways of trading. They thought Luciano was the man to do this, despite his arrest and conviction in 1936, which meant he ran the organization and led from behind bars.

The Demise of the Mangano Brothers

The meeting may have gone well, but, in real life, the forties was a time of shifting allegiances, plotting, backstabbing, power struggles, and treachery. When Luciano was paroled in 1946, he immediately returned to his homeland Sicily. He already knew the writing was on the wall for his leadership and Costello and Genovese were both vying for the position. While they didn't directly affect the Mangano family, Vincent knew New York was a firecracker of a place filled with younger wannabe bosses, and he felt the pressure.

Vincent was in his sixties and knew his underboss Anastasia was waiting to step into his shoes. In 1951, the body of Vincent's brother Philip was found dressed in his underwear and a shirt with three small bullet wounds on his neck and cheeks. There had been rumors he was talking to the feds, so the execution seemed to have been carried out by hitmen, and the police were eager to talk to Vincent.

They may have been eager, but Vincent had disappeared, and nobody seemed to know where he was. It didn't take a genius to work out that Vincent had joined his brother in the afterlife, but nobody was talking. Anastasia had formed links with Frank Costello, who had taken Luciano's position as the head of the family, and he recognized the skills he brought to the Cosa Nostra. Costello was known as "The Prime minister" because of his suave and polished demeanor. He mixed with ease in the company of politicians and public officials and garnered their trust.

Costello consulted only with Anastasia and cut Mangano out of the loop, which made him angry. He and his brother may have been making noises about leaving the life of the mob, and this meant they couldn't be trusted. There are reports that Vincent turned to his friends, Joe Bonanno and Joe Profaci, for help, but they turned their back on him. Did Anastasia order the hit on Vincent and Philip? Probably, but he would only have done so with the full backing of the Committee.

Vincent Mangano's body was never found, and his killers were never named. Still, there is an interesting piece of text in an autobiography of Anastasia written by his former mob alliance member, Frank DiMatteo, part of the crew that ran Red Hook, which was the favored territory of Anastasia. The story relates a conversation between himself and "Uncle Joe" Bonanno about killing Mangano. It claims that, rather than ordering the hit on Mangano, Anastasia had carried out the killing. He had heard that Mangano was planning to take out a contract on him and decided it was time to get his hands dirty again just to see the expression on Vincent's face as he took his last breath.

Albert contacted Costello and Luciano to get their permission and was given it immediately. The story was that Anastasia arranged to meet with Vincent at a deserted warehouse on Columbia St. to pick up some funds from a local gambling racket. Apparently (according to Matteo), Vincent entered the warehouse with a smile on his face and his arms outstretched when Albert shot him in the head and the chest. There was no showdown or dramatic dialogue, just a clean shot that killed Mangano immediately. Then DiMatteo asked Joe why the body had never been found, and he replied nobody bothered looking for him because they all thought he was hiding. When asked where the body was, Joe smiled and described the scene. "They gutted him at sea and fitted him with concrete shoes. He looked like a mummy!"

CHAPTER 5:
The Anastasia Era

The murder of a boss went against everything the Committee stood for, even though they may have given permission, and Lucky Luciano had to be seen to bring Anastasia to task for the murders. There is a chance that no permission was given, which is the view held by some of the other family members, and that Anastasia killed Mangano to become the boss of the family by breaking one of the cardinal rules of the Cosa Nostra.

There was a sit-down organized, and Anastasia was asked about the murders. Without admitting anything, he raised the point that Mangano had been plotting to kill him and that any hit on him would have been justified under the organization's rules. He claimed that, even if he had done it and said he hadn't, it was a clear case of kill or be killed. Joe Bonanno was left as head of the Commission when it was clear Mangano wasn't coming back. Still, the fact was this well-known maniac psychopath now had a seat on the Commission. Anastasia was officially named the head of the Mangano family, which became the Anastasia family.

Costello was facing pressure from other branches of the Cosa Nostra as Vito Genovese was making a play for his job, and he needed the muscle and support he would garner from Anastasia. His former muscle man was Willie Moretti, who ran a dedicated group of over fifty men, but he was suffering severe symptoms of syphilis that had been left untreated and was no longer in possession of his facilities. The word was put out that Morelli was a liability and needed to be "put to sleep" for his own sake and the good of the organization.

Suppose Costello was behind Anastasia carrying out the hit on Mangano. That would explain why he didn't face any consequences and started his reign as head of the family with little resistance. Anastasia may have gone down in history as a more colorful character in mob stories. Still, he wasn't as effective as Mangano, and his appointment signaled the demise of the old-school Mafia and a more populist and notorious era for the Cosa Nostra.

Mangano vs. Anastasia

Comparing the two bosses helps to highlight this fact:

- Mangano was boss for twenty years and never went to prison, while Anastasia served time before being promoted and was more than likely heading there before he was killed.

- Mangano made profits, not headlines. The only picture of him is in the crime scene, one of his body, but Anastasia courted press attention and made the Cosa Nostra part of the media. He loved his notoriety, and as soon as he became boss, he ordered a hit on a "civilian," which led to intense scrutiny from the media.

- Mangano was a hands-off boss and trusted his underlings to carry out the dirty work, like murder and violence, which insulated his position. He may not have liked Anastasia, but he recognized his skills and strengths and put them to use. He was a classic delegator, who knew his family needed him to stay out of prison and the news. Anastasia relished the violent side of the business and would often be implicated in the hits, even when he was made boss. He drew heat from the law and raised the number of murder victims during his short reign.

- Mangano followed the commandments of the Cosa Nostra to the letter. He had principles and stuck to protocol religiously while Anastasia flew by the seat of his pants, relying on his close ties to Luciano to keep him safe. He regularly broke the rules, ratted on his compatriots, and threw people under the bus to save his own skin.

Vincent Mangano may have been forgotten in the bigger picture, but he played his part in making the family stronger. However, we are in the Anastasia era, and this is his story.

The Murder Inc. Incident

We have alluded to the fall of Murder Inc. following the defection of Kid Twist Reles. He sent six of his fellow hitmen to Ol' Sparky at Sing prison, but when he implicated Albert Anastasia, he failed to make the witness stand and fell to his death while under police guard. Reles was being kept in a second-floor bedroom at the Half Moon Hotel in Coney Island, awaiting the trial of Anastasia, when he was found dead under his hotel window. There were bedsheets found, which seemed to indicate he was trying to escape, but speculation arose that he was pushed to his death by the officer watching over him.

The police officers guarding him were demoted, and the trial was canceled due to a lack of witnesses. Rumors flew that NYPD Detective Burns was on the payroll of the mob and was responsible for the death of Reles, but a grand jury decided his death should be ruled accidental. He is buried in Queens, and he was given the amusing nickname, "The canary that could sing but couldn't fly."

What did emerge was that, because of his tie and connections, Anastasia was like Teflon; nothing stuck to him. During the time that Reles was talking to the law, many prominent gangsters fled

America and returned to Italy, but Albert stayed defiant to the end. He had built a sprawling estate in Fort Lee, New Jersey, with stunning views of New York, and claimed it was his oasis of calm in a city of chaos.

Anastasias Fort Lee Home

If ever a home reflected its owner, Fort Lee was Anastasia to a tee. It was a mansion filled with false walls, tunnels that led under the floors, and several slaughter rooms fitted with easy-to-clean walls and drains on the floor. Anastasia maintained that he liked to hunt, and these rooms were for "dressing deer," but most people knew what happened down there was far grislier than deer dressing. The estate fences were so secure that the gangsters visiting the property were told to steer clear or risk losing a body part to the dogs that patrolled there.

Interesting Fact

Anastasia's home has become a real estate headache as other properties in the area have been sold for over $18 million. His grisly mansion was sold recently for just over five million dollars. He would probably chuckle at the fact that his grisly reputation made the home so unappealing seventy years after his demise.

Anastasia Finally Gets His Just Desserts

As the fifties progressed, Anastasia's luck seemed to have run out. In 1952, he ordered a hit on a man for his part in the capture of the bank robber Willie Sutton. This went against all Cosa Nostra rules and made the mob headline fodder once more. The families banded together and voiced their outrage, citing Anastasia had overstepped the boundaries once more. Albert had also made an enemy of Meyer Lansky, a close associate of Luciano, when he opened a chain of casinos in Cuba in direct competition with Lansky's casinos that had been operating under the protection of the Cosa Nostra for years.

This blatant snub led to Lansky and Vito Genovese, another man who wasn't a fan of Anastasia, hatching a plot to replace Albert with Carlo Gambino, a prominent member steadily rising through the ranks. He promised him the leadership of the Anastasia family if he helped them get rid of Albert. Meanwhile, Frank Costello had survived an attempt on his life in May 1957, which led to his resignation as the boss of the family. The attempt was a plan by Genovese and Gambino to kill Costello and take control of his faction, but it spurred him to join forces with Anastasia and regain power.

They decided Costello was insignificant and could be allowed to live, but Anastasia needed to be taken out of the equation. In October 1957, the plan came to fruition when he was chauffeured from his Fort Lee home to his favored barber shop at the Sheraton Hotel in downtown Manhattan and sat in his favorite chair for a haircut. Two masked gunmen entered the barber shop and fired shots into the back of the stunned mob boss. His bodyguard had left the scene to take a walk around the block, and Albert was left vulnerable to attack.

The gunmen fired ten bullets into the mob boss, and even though he attempted to fight back, he mistook the image of the gunmen in the mirror as the real thing and ended up crashing through the glass, causing more horrendous injuries. The gunmen disappeared into the city and were never named or identified. Mob lore refuses to name them or the people who ordered the hit, but the Genovese name must be included in a list of potential suspects.

So, Albert had finally missed the signs that he had pushed important people too far. The image of his lifeless body partially covered with towels from the barber shop is an iconic part of mob history and became the image that defined the violent inter-family feuding of the 1950s. Changes were coming, and Albert's death marked the end of his thirty-year influence on the mob. His legacy was about to give way to the Gambino family, who was to become the most powerful crime syndicate in history.

Albert Anastasia: Terrifying Facts about the Most Terrifying Crime Figures in History

- The former FBI assistant director James Kallstrom was tasked with discovering how many murders could be linked to Anastasia. He reported it was unquestionably in the thousands and possibly tens of thousands. The exact figure never has and will probably never be known.

- Anastasia was the hitman of the era and earned a variety of nicknames, including "Lord High Executioner," "The Mad Hatter," and "The One-Man Army," of which he was inordinately proud.

- He had eleven siblings, eight brothers, and three sisters, and a year before prohibition, he arrived in America with three of his brothers illegally to begin their mob life.

- Albert married Elsa Barnet and had just one son, named Anthony Jr.

- Just two years after arriving in America, Anastasia was convicted of murder and sentenced to death. He spent two years on Death Row before being granted a retrial in 1922. When the case came to court, the witnesses for the prosecution had mysteriously disappeared. Albert walked free and escaped the shadow of the electric chair.

- The year after, he was arrested for firearm charges and spent two years behind bars establishing a web of connections to prominent gangsters.

- Anastasia was the mastermind of the plan to gain a pardon for the imprisoned Luciano by using his ties to the docks to aid the war effort. He also used his Sicilian ties to help the American war effort in Italy, which eventually led to parole for the jailed mobster.

- As the Murder Inc. investigation hit the headlines, he decided to enlist to avoid the heat. He served until 1943 and was rewarded for his efforts with citizenship in the US and an honorable discharge.

A Cameo of the Little King of Garbage, Vincent Squillante

Certain mob members have been portrayed in the media and written about so much that we feel they are a part of history, and we know who they were and how they operated. However, the early history of mob life wasn't that well-documented, and many stories from the early days are based on rumors and word-of-mouth accounts about the workings of the Mafia and the Cosa Nostra.

Al Capone, Lucky Luciano, Albert Anastasia, and other members of the mob have become folk heroes. Although they were criminals and violent murderers, they didn't interfere with civilians and kept their business within the organization. Is a folk hero the right term to use? Some criminals have gained a form of respect from the people who watch their antics on film and secretly enjoy their rebellious streak, wishing they had that excitement in their life. Of course, we know these individuals were murderous villains who lived by their own rules and what they stood for wasn't moral or righteous. Still, in the same respect, we must acknowledge their code of honor existed, even though it was repellant to most law-abiding citizens.

Vincent Squillante isn't part of the mainstream history of the mob, but he is the perfect person to provide a snapshot into the life of the average mobster and a time during an era that will never happen again. Very little was known about the underworld activities of Italian/American organized crime activities before 1951, when the Kefauver Hearings were published. This was an 11,000-page report on the Mafia and how the organization operated. It included details of mob life never before made public. The public was informed about the profits and dealings the mob conducted in various cities and how they used narcotics to fund their organization. The report was the first time the public had been made aware of how relevant organized crime was, and it wasn't just the subject of movies and TV shows.

Vincent Squillante and his time in the mob is a typical tale of a boy born to poor immigrant parents in the US and facing a choice between low-paid labor and life in the Bronx or the seemingly profitable life of a gangster. Put yourself in his shoes, a teenage boy who grew up in a crowded house with his parents and at least nine siblings with no prospects and seemingly no way to escape his life of poverty. With his diminutive stature and slight build, he was reportedly just 5'2" in height and weighed less than 120lbs, which meant he couldn't get physically demanding jobs, and he was destined to work in retail or a factory. When he met mob boss Frank Scalice, he must have thought his luck had changed, especially when the boss of the Mangano family proposed and backed Vincent's introduction to the mob. He may not have been the typical gangster type, but because he was the same size as a jockey didn't mean he had nothing to bring to the table. Although his patronage by Scalice hasn't been confirmed, if it is true, it makes what happened next more like a Greek tragedy than a tale from New York.

What happened during the 1930s to Squillante wasn't documented. Still, it is believed he was a member of a crew working in the Bronx alongside other low-level soldiers, like Nanny the Geep, Pasta Fazula, and Joey Surprise. It isn't known which specific crew he ran with, but he did seem close to Rocco Mazzie and Davis Amodeo, two of the crew bosses at the time. Some people believe the gangsters of that era gave themselves nicknames to make themselves seem more charismatic, but the reality is much more mundane. They lived in a world where men often didn't know each other's given names because they didn't trust others not to rat on them. This was a world of secrecy and shadows, and it made sense to keep your anonymity.

Squillante first attracted the attention of the law in the early '50s, when he was charged with tax evasion, extortion, and drug offenses. He was given a hefty fine for his tax evasion, but the other charges were dropped. At that time, he was responsible for several distribution companies, and he increased their levies to pay his fines, which didn't go down well with his crew members. Mafia members were always supposed to pay their way, and if they were fined, it was their responsibility to pay, not to pass the debt on to other people.

The family we now know as the Gambinos may have had years of turmoil and name-changing in the early part of their history. Still, they did have three consistent sources of legitimate income, the waterfront, construction, and garbage. Vincent wasn't a killer or a violent mobster, but he was smart and made his money for the

Mafia by controlling the garbage side of the business and making the family a stack of cash.

He operated from his office in Long Island City and Manhattan, where he used the Teamsters union to grow his empire. He collaborated with a crooked con man named Bernie Adelstein, who had been running the union since its creation and had established Mafia connections. As the secretary and treasurer of the Teamsters, Adelstein worked with Squillante to force nonunion firms to join them, and the pair targeted any garbage operators who failed to come on board and put them out of business. They soon formed a monopoly and used artificially low prices to outbid their remaining rivals until Squillante emerged as the Czar of Garbage or the self-proclaimed Little King of Garbage.

A senate committee called him and Adelstein to testify in 1958, and although they tried to get the pair to talk, their efforts fell on deaf ears. They refused to answer all 120 questions the chairman threw at them, and Squillante even consulted his lawyer before admitting his name. The committee questioned the pair on their links with four carting companies and the nefarious way they operated. They concluded that he was a powerhouse in Mafia circles, but they couldn't charge him with anything.

At the time, Anastasia and Mangano were still battling it out at the head of the family, and in 1951, we know things changed when Mangano was killed by gunmen, reportedly under the orders of Albert. Anastasia was now the boss, and although Squillante was rumored to be a hitman for the new boss, there is no evidence to back up these facts. Anastasia may have been a violent psychopath, but he realized the mob was a business, and Squillante brought a lot of money to the family. Squillante was tight with the boss, but was he tight enough to be trusted with the hit on Frank Scalice, who was the underboss to Anastasia?

Scalice was the man who introduced Squillante to the mob, but was he one of the shooters who took out this popular underboss on a hot afternoon in June 1957? Scalice was shopping for fruit at a store in the Bronx when two men approached him in the store. Witnesses report that both men were dressed identically in crisp white shirts and black trousers, and both wore sunglasses. They walked up to the mob underboss and shot him five times in the chest, face, and head before leaving the store, climbing into a waiting car, disappearing into the shimmering heat of the afternoon, and driving away.

It was a well-known fact that Scalice had a fixed routine, and every Monday, he had lunch in the Bronx at Anne and Tony's Italian restaurant, where he would share mozzarella and roasted peppers with his brother, Giacomo. The latter ran a candy shop in the area. After lunch, Frank would stroll down the street and chat with the locals, often stopping to admire babies in their strollers and talking to older men sitting in the sun. He loved to share stories of their times in the old country and would often be seen passing them a few bucks to get their groceries. He would then stop at the grocery store to buy some fruit.

The store was the perfect place for a hit. Being easy to enter and exit made the gunmen's job easier, and even though a patrol car was on the scene in minutes, there was little chance of capture, and the shooters got a clean getaway. Did Squillante carry out the hit? Probably not, but he would have been aware of it and may even have arranged the hitmen to cement his place in Anastasia's favor.

Squillante continued to run his garbage empire and thrived under the reign of Anastasia. He continued working with Adelstein, and his brother Nunzio also climbed through the ranks. Mob life was good for him, and he shared a special relationship with Anastasia, to the point that he claimed the mob boss had made him an honorary godson, although there was no evidence to back up his claim. What was known is that, often, when Anastasia was visiting his local barber for a haircut, Squillante would join him, and the pair would shoot the breeze in their separate barber's chairs. This fact would become especially poignant to Vincent when, in 1957, Anastasia was killed as he had a haircut while Vince was seated in his chair. As the bullets flew, a manicurist told police that Vince yelled, "I'm outta here!" and left his boss to his fate.

1957 was a pivotal year for the Gambino family. The era of psychopath murders and blood feuds was behind them, and the new boss Carlo Gambino brought calm to the family. He did have a few loose ends to tie up, and Vince must have been nervous as the new boss arrived. When he was arrested in November 1957, Squillante must have been unsure that his new family would have his back as they had in the past. He faced serious charges of extortion that arose when he and his companies tried to use their regular tactics to obtain a garbage contract for the local US air base. He may have survived family retribution, but the law had finally caught up with him, and he was given a fifteen-year sentence for his part in the extortion racket.

While he was languishing in jail, awaiting his appeal process, Squillante was sharing a cell with a Russian spy named Rudolf Abel, who was actually an Englishman from the northeast of the country. Squillante was outraged at his cellmate and claimed his presence was a "cruel and unusual punishment" for him and that his association with the spy was ruining his good name. Eventually, Squillante was released on bail and returned to the streets of New York, where he promptly disappeared in September 1960. The official word from the mob was that he had gone underground to avoid the law. Still, most people recognized Gambino ordered a hit on him to stop the possibility of him turning state evidence and revealing the mob's involvement in the waste industry. The truth was that, when Anastasia was taken out of the equation, Squillante wasn't part of the plans for the Gambino family. They couldn't risk him turning on them and becoming an informant.

His demise is typically part of the rumor mill that surrounds the Mafia, with some sources reporting he was invited to a party where he got very drunk and was then left in a room with all the wives and girlfriends of the men he had ordered to be killed. They reportedly stabbed him repeatedly and chopped up the body before it was taken to some unknown resting place. A police informant told the cops he was killed by a group of mobsters, including his former friend Joey Surprise, and then his body was compacted and dumped at the garbage tip.

Was the Little King of Garbage always destined to become part of the business he had run so successfully, or does the thought of a group of angry spouses sound more plausible? That's the fascinating part of mob lore; you will probably never know, and you can choose which story to believe. Squillante wasn't the most glamorous mobster, but he does represent the ethos of the Mafia throughout the ages. The shifting sands and the clean-up operation that happens when a mob boss is replaced are often messy and violent. Vacuums are created, and new blood is needed to fill trusted positions, which means some people will fall foul of the new regime. Loyalty is only rewarded when it is given to the current leader; when it is misplaced, it can be deadly.

Perhaps the most amusing part of the story must be the outrage Squillante showed when he was in prison with a suspected Russian spy. Did the members of the Mafia believe themselves above regular criminals? It would seem so, and that mindset sums up the importance in which they held themselves and still do today.

CHAPTER 6:

The Boss of All Bosses – Carlo Gambino

As we reach the halfway point of the history of the mob, changes are apparent. The old ways are receding, and the new Mafia/Cosa Nostra is regrouping and changing. With the death of Anastasia, it was time to treat the organization more like a business than a personal killing machine and concentrate on profits rather than body counts. Step forward, Carlo Gambino, the man who gave the notorious family its modern-day name and shaped it to become the organization we know today.

If somebody wanted to get an overview of Carlo Gambino, they would just have to watch the classic mob movie *The Godfather* and the character of Vito Corleone. Short in stature and with a prominent nose, Gambino wasn't your typical mobster. He was always seen with a disarming grin and a friendly demeanor, which threw his opponents off guard when they first met. Even when he was arrested and had his mug shot taken, a wry grin would dominate his features and give the impression that he was just an ordinary Joe and not the Godfather figure he was.

The Apalachin Meeting

Following the death of Anastasia, Gambino took over the family and renamed it. In contrast, Vito Genovese took control of the Luciano crime family following the wounding and subsequent retirement of Costello. He decided it was time for a new way of organizing the families and combining the interests of all American Cosa Nostra factions with other groups from Italy and Cuba. He organized the Apalachin Meeting to take place in New York at the home of notorious mobster, Joe the Barber, who was the leader of the Buffalino crime family. Apalachin was a sleepy hamlet, and the authorities already knew some suspicious activities had taken place at Barbara's estate the previous year.

One eagle-eyed state trooper had looked at records from 1956 and discovered that Carmine "The Cigar" Galante's vehicle had been stopped for a minor issue. After checking his license, it was discovered he was driving with fake documents and had an extensive criminal record in New York and other districts of America. They placed surveillance on the estate and noticed disturbing activities happening. They knew Barbara's son was booking rooms in local hotels and motels, and there was a flurry of activity at the estate. Large quantities of meat and fish were being delivered, and some very expensive vehicles were spotted passing through town and parking at the estate.

A meeting had been arranged so the most important Mafia and Cosa Nostra figures could get together to discuss how the rackets run by the recently deceased Anastasia would be distributed between the five families and the possible uprising of two prominent capos, Aniello Dellacroce and Armand Rava. They were there to discuss the gambling and narcotic ties the Cosa Nostra had with Cuba and how to make them more secure.

The Sicilian Mafia was in town and staying at a local hotel called the Grand Hotel, and the town was buzzing to see these original gangster types in sleepy Apalachin. Top leaders, like Bonanno, Galante, Grafola, and other notorious Mafia bosses, were spotted at the estate and in the town, which meant the authorities knew something was going on. They needed to get their troops together to raid the estate. They set up a blockade on the road leading to the estate, but a late arrival, one of the Sicilian factions, spotted the roadblock and alerted the rest of the Mafia members already at the meeting.

Over a hundred men fled the estate, and fifty escaped without capture, but sixty were stopped and questioned. The main hitters and Commission members were questioned but claimed they were in town to visit Joe because they had heard he was ill. Others weren't so lucky, and they were apprehended and charged with the crime of "lying about the nature of an underworld venture," a charge that sounded hollow even to the most dedicated lawman.

The Aftermath of the Meeting

Members of the Gambino family were arrested alongside family members from other factions. These included the NE Pennsylvania, Bonanno, Genovese, Lucchese, Profaci, DeCavalcante, Buffalo, Utica, Rochester, Pittsburgh, and many others who felt the pressure coming from the top of the law enforcement agencies.

Carlo Gambino and four of his caporegimes were indicted and found guilty of the crimes with which they were charged. The sentences ranged from three to five years of incarceration and a ten thousand dollar fine. The prison sentences were overturned the following year on appeal.

While the meeting was a damp squib as far as getting the organization together, it was significant in other ways. The long-time leader of the FBI, J. Edgar Hoover, had been in denial for decades about the existence of a National Crime Syndicate and the need to crack down on Mafia and mob activities. He couldn't continue to ignore them any more following the Apalachin meeting and the press coverage it attracted.

The Top Hoodlum Program

He created the "Top Hoodlum Program" and swore to bring down all the top family bosses across the country. This wasn't the first attempt to crack down on organized crime, but it was the most publicized. In 1933, Chicago agents had monitored the rise of criminal activities and the existence of over three hundred members of the Mafia in their area, and they predicted the rise of underground activities and their rackets.

John Dillinger was the name on everyone's lips in the 1930s, and his violent crimes and subsequent manhunt signaled the way the underworld was becoming more powerful. They had rackets that produced income in all forms of business; even the more unconventional businesses were feeling the pressure. Dentists, shopkeepers, and even manufacturing outlets were forced to pay protection money, and the law seemed powerless to stop the extortion.

The Biography of Carlo Gambino

Born in 1902 in Palermo, Sicily, Carlo was destined for the Mafia life due to his family ties. At that time, the organization was known as the "Honored Society," which may sound reputable. However, it represented a bunch of criminals, who deified the law in an organized manner, leading to the term "organized crime." As he grew up in Italy, the leader of the country, President Mussolini, was going after the more renowned Nafia members and chasing them out of the country. Carlo made the most of the organized crime faction in Italy and, in 1921, became a "made man," which meant he was part of the rapidly growing organization and becoming more powerful.

Carlo may have looked like your regular teenager with his handsome face and winning smile, but he was a stone-cold killer before he reached the age of twenty. Details are sketchy, but it was common knowledge that nobody was granted the honor of "made man" without at least one kill under their belt. Carlo had strong allies in Italy, and his brother-in-law was a respected gangster and commanded a level of fear with which Carlo would also become associated. His brother Paolo was just as committed as Carlo to life, while his other brother Gaspare managed to break away from society.

When the pressure from the Italian authorities proved too much for the criminal fraternity, Carlo joined the exodus to America in 1921. He landed in Norfolk, Virginia, where he sent out messages to his relatives and considered his options. Because he was an illegal immigrant, he joined his cousin in New York and became part of the established Mafia society that was thriving in that area. He chose the D'Aquila family and gave them his allegiance. As part of the five families, Carlo was identified with the gang culture known as the "Young Turks" and formed important ties with the other members of the group.

The Young Turks were a group of Italian Jewish men who were respectful of the Mustache Pete brigade, but they signaled the future for the mob. Frank Scalice and Vito Genovese were showing promise and later played important roles in the organization, and Gambino was their friend and compatriot. They formed part of the future in waiting and knew their time would come.

During the Castellammarese War, the Young Turks watched as the old brigade fought between themselves, and the Masseria and Maranzano families brought about their own destruction. The bodies piled higher and higher as the streets of New York ran with the blood of mobsters. The war was a turning point for the Irish and Jewish factions of the Mafia. They realized the old way of thinking was being eradicated, and the Sicilian and Italian mobsters soon realized the future of the Mafia lay in working with other nationalities and broadening the membership.

Carlo was part of the group of Mafioso that put a stop to the war and formed the new Commission formed to make sure it never happened again. Luciano may have been the main man, but Gambino knew the power of anonymity. He was a low-key part of the organization and maintained a persona of a regular family man with his modest home and seemingly normal life. The new mafia system suited him well; his intelligence and cunning meant he could operate multiple rackets and rake in cash without having to resort to violence.

Gambino ran his activities well and was well-respected by his men. He thrived during WWII by running his regular rackets and a successful sideline selling ration stamps on the black market. Carlo was content with his lot during the reign of Albert Anastasia and had no aspirations to become the boss; anonymity suited him. However, in the late 1950s, Anastasia became a liability to the organization, culminating in his hit on a civilian named Shuster that broke all the Cosa Nostra rules.

The committee and the other families knew that, if Anastasia continued, they would all be under intensified scrutiny from the law, and that was bad for the organization. They turned to Gambino as a loyal member and asked him to organize a hit on Anastasia, and mafia history was made in a barber shop in 1957. Gambino took leadership of the family and was proclaimed the Godfather. His methods differed greatly from Anastasia's, and his leadership led to wealth and prosperity for the family that couldn't have been achieved under any other boss.

Gambino knew he needed to expand and distribute the influence his family had all around the world. He branched out and brought hundreds of millions of dollars to the family coffers. Money means power in the Cosa Nostra, and Gambino became one of the world's most powerful and respected bosses. The rest of the Young Turks dominated the headlines but soon fell foul of the law, and, by the late 60s, most were dead or in prison. Carlo carried on regardless.

Even though he was the subject of surveillance by the FBI throughout his reign, they never pinned anything on him. Other Mafia leaders fell by the wayside and became the victims of assassinations or arrests, many arranged by Carlo, but he continued to be the Godfather for decades. He was tight-lipped and careful, and even when they arrested him in 1970, he maintained his smiling demeanor, and they had to release him due to lack of evidence.

Dominic Scialo

Some people mistakenly underestimated the Godfather and thought of him as a kindly older man. Gambino was feared and respected by most members of the Cosa Nostra, and they knew it was essential not to speak out of turn. Dominic Scialo was a well-liked 46-year-old member of the Colombo family, who was experiencing mental health issues and was a heavy drinker. He was known as the "King of Coney Island," but his reign was short-lived when he drunkenly insulted Carlo in a restaurant in New York. He had to be removed by several of Gambino's thugs while the Godfather remained calm and smiled. Two days later, the body of

Scialo was found encased in concrete with a bullet hole in his head. The message was sent.

The Death of Gambino

After the Scialo killing in 1974, Gambino resumed his role as head of the family for another two years before his death in 1976 following a heart attack. He died a peaceful death at his home on Long Island and was buried in a local cemetery. He was eulogized in the *New York Times* as the most powerful Mafia Boss ever, who had a strong influence on the labor unions and played a huge part in the concerns of the longshoremen. He was remembered as a kindly-looking figure, who looked more like your favorite uncle than a cold-blooded killer who ran his family with an iron rod.

True Facts about Carlo Gambino

1. When he died, he was in a "state of grace" due to having been given the last rites by a Catholic priest. He was a Roman Catholic, who was associated with the Jewish faction of the Mafia.

2. He was known as an "Original" because of his association with founder members of the "Honored Society," including Paul Castellano.

3. When he arrived in the US on the SS Vincenzo Florio, he was the only passenger on board and ate only olives and drank wine for the month-long journey.

4. Gambino rackets flourished in Chicago, LA, Boston, and multiple other cities, even though they had powerful bosses in place.

5. During the '60s, the Gambino family made approximately $500 million annually and ran thirty crews across the country.

6. Carlo's son Tommy married the daughter of the boss of the Gagliano family, forming a powerful alliance and friendship.

7. When Lucky Luciano died in 1962, Gambino gave a moving eulogy at his funeral in Queens, New York. He spoke about their friendship and closeness and called him a close companion.

8. When the FBI organized a surveillance van to park outside his house, Gambino still conducted his business using sign language, codes, and other ways to avoid being recorded.

9. One conversation between Gambino and his associates was a series of sentences that contained two words, frogs' legs!

10. He died immediately after watching the Yankees win the American League pennant and was buried next to his wife, who had died three years earlier.

CHAPTER 7:
The Castellano Regime

Just before his death, Carlo Gambino named his successor, Paul Castellano, which irked the underboss, Neil Dellacroce, and angered a rising mobster, John Gotti . Castellano was an imposing figure, who looked like your typical brother-in-law, and the two men shared a close friendship. Was he the obvious choice for the position of the boss after Carlo passed away? Maybe not for some, but he looked the part and had the experience.

Castellanos Early Life

Paul was born in 1915 in Manhattan in the US and was the youngest son of Guiseppe, who was a member of the Mangano family that later became the Gambino family. He spent his early years learning the butchering trade and helping his father collect gambling receipts from the rackets being run in the area. His sister was also helpful in the butcher shop, but she avoided any Mafia-related activities.

His first brush with the law was for robbery. He and two associates robbed a hardware store, and Paul was caught as he tried to escape. His two assistants got away, and the police pressured Castellano to name them to receive a reduced sentence. Castellano refused, and because he stayed silent, he received a harsh three-month sentence for the robbery. Paul was gaining a reputation for loyalty and keeping his promises, which harked back to the earlier rules of the Cosa Nostra and the vow to keep the family safe. It seemed like a natural progression for Paul to follow in his father's footsteps, become a madman, and join the Mangano family.

He came to the attention of boss Anastasia and earned the rank of caporegime, quite a high rank for such a young man. As the reign of Gambino progressed, he made himself part of the team that Carlo relied upon to keep the family prosperous and safe from the law. Castellano was an attendant of the infamous Apalachin meeting when the big bosses of the Mafia met to discuss certain information and create a new template for the organization. Paul didn't manage to get away from the police raid and was arrested and charged with "withholding information and taking part in underworld activities" and was given a five-year sentence for his part in the meeting.

Castellano insisted he was at the meeting as part of his job as the President of the Allied Butchers Association in Brooklyn. Because he was legitimately a trained butcher and was involved in Dial Poultry, a legal business, the police couldn't make the charges stick. They offered him release and anonymity for his testimony, but Castellano stuck to his guns despite spending a year in prison before the charge was overturned. He earned points from the higher-up members of the organization for his steadfast refusal to testify.

He was quoted as saying, *"It doesn't matter how many bibles you put your hand on, there are certain promises you make that are more sacred than any court of law,"* a creed that Castellano lived up to with fervor.

The Concrete Club

One of the most profitable arms of the Gambino family business was their involvement in a consortium of Mafia families, known as the Concrete Club. Castellano was strongly opposed to drug trafficking but was interested in another form of white powder, concrete. The construction business was one of the most lucrative in New York in the eighties and seemed an obvious target for mob interest. As far back as the 1930s, the mob had been involved in construction, and the five families employed their regular tactics to gain income and control the city. Following the Great Depression, the contractors considered the mob influence a 'necessary evil.' They recognized their control meant they had labor and supplies to ensure they could get their work done on schedule. The mob had such control they could shut down and call a halt to building work and the distribution of essential materials.

The 1980s saw an expansion of the construction industry, resulting in a more dedicated organization run by the mob to oversee the filtering of profits and the chance to make even more cash from contractors and their suppliers. They were named the Concrete Club, and Castellano was a designated member representing the Gambino family. Why did construction offer so many chances to make money? The construction industry in New York at the time was multi-faceted and came with complicated legal requirements and contracts.

Public and private projects meant great swathes of people were involved, from laying the foundations to the construction, installing the utilities and the interior design, and then selling the property. Mob connections helped contractors push through legal requirements, and for a fee, they would make sure projects got signed off, even if they failed to meet building regulations. It was widely acknowledged that the materials used in mob construction risked being below par and even dangerous, as the materials they used would be watered down or replaced by sub-par alternatives. Castellano and the Gambino family also used their Teamster contacts to delay any projects that failed to pay their fee to ensure smooth working conditions.

These projects were often subject to other forms of unlawful activities, with workers stealing materials to make a quick buck and the contractors cutting corners. They were failing to pay their dues, and this affected the funds available for public contracts, like roads, schools, and other important parts of the New York infrastructure. While certain contractors, like Stanley Sternchos and possibly Donald Trump, were firmly involved with the mob and accepted the extra fees as standard, other contractors were determined to work with the law enforcement agencies to end the grip the mob had on construction. Although the FBI and Rudy Guiliani eventually came down heavily on the Concrete Club, Castellano was already out of the loop. He had become boss of the Gambino family in 1976 and had other fish to fry.

1975 was a busy year for Castellano. He was charged with loansharking, but the police failed to make the charges stick, and once more, Paul stayed schtum about his mob connections. 1975 was also the year he gained the nickname "the Chicken Man" when he had his daughter's boyfriend killed for comparing the gangster to Frank Perdue, who was a spokesperson for the poultry industry. He gave the contract to a member of the Bonanno family, and Vito Borelli was shot and killed on his orders.

Castellanos Succession

Gambino had clarified that he favored his brother-in-law for the top job but wanted his underboss, Neil Delacroce, to remain in his current position as the underboss to Castellano. Although Dellacroce attended the succession meeting, he was imprisoned for tax evasion shortly after and mounted no formal protest at the succession. However, the damage had been done, and the family split into two factions that barely managed to function under the new leadership.

Castellano immediately began to change the way the Gambino family ran the business and halted all narcotics and any crimes involving violence against women. He was criminally conservative and preferred to run the family like a CEO rather than a mob boss and invest in legitimate businesses. He still benefited from profits from loansharking, gambling, and other illegal activities, but he recognized that legitimate businesses would attract less attention from the law. Despite his penchant for the legality, Castellano recognized the need to assert his leadership, and in 1978, he made a decision that would further split the family.

Nicky Scibetta was a drunk and an addict, but he had important family ties within the Gambino family. He was the brother-in-law of Sammy the bull Gravano, who was a rising force in the family. When Castellano ordered a hit on Scibetta, Gravano stated he would kill Castellano first rather than agree with the hit. Scibetta had been involved in various public fights and had insulted the daughter of prominent gangster George DeCicco. DeCicco convinced Gravano that the hit was legitimate and accepted that death was a suitable punishment for Scibetta's actions, and the contract was then carried out.

In the same year, Castello decided he needed to take out a father and son team that was causing him grief, known as the Eppolito Sr. and Jr. team. The pair had approached him asking permission to take out Nino Gaggi, a prominent capo in the family with a strong tie to Roy De Meo and a favorite of Castellano, because he was infringing on their territory, attempting to take over their rackets. Paul gave him a vague answer and told him he would consider the contract, but he immediately warned Gaggi that the pair were gunning for him. Gaggi and his trusted soldier DeMeo killed the pair on the same day as the Pope came to the Big Apple.

Eppolito Jr. had been an embarrassment to the family and lost the family thousands of dollars on a drug deal that went wrong. He was also implicated in a charity fraud with some important backers, and Castellano didn't appreciate the attention the press showed to the scam. After the crime family had been linked by the TV program *60 Minutes*, it was time to take out the father and son outfit for good. The pair were invited to the home of an old-time gangster Pete Piacente for a sit-down to resolve the issues they had raised. On route to the venue, with DeMeo and Gaggi in the car with them, the Senior Eppolito must have had a feeling of doom and instructed his son to pull over to use the bathroom at the local gas station.

As he pulled the Thunderbird to a halt, the two other men pulled out their guns and shot Eppolito Sr. and Jr. in the head, killing them instantly. The case was investigated by a member of their family, who had taken a different route and joined the police officers. Louis Eppolito was a highly respected detective in the NYPD. He was philosophical about losing his relatives, saying, "That's the life they chose," and attempting to solve the case. As with most mob hits, he found a wall of silence waiting for him, and although he went to the morgue to see the bodies and wash them, he later returned to his duties as a protector of the Pope and ran alongside his vehicle. Louis Eppolito would later be the 11th most decorated cop in NY history.

In 1978, Castellano formed important alliances with the Irish faction of the Mafia, known as the Westies and the Sicilian brothers in New Jersey, to form an army of killers to help him take control of New York and carry out his contracts. While the Sicilian Brothers were known for their ties to narcotics, Castellano recognized their worth and made the Cherry Hill Gambino part of his army.

With this army in place, Castellano became more reclusive and built himself a lavish home in the popular district of Todt Hill in Staten Island. Like some of his former bosses, he believed he should have the best of the best when it came to his home, and his seventeen-room home looked like the White House and contained an Olympic-sized swimming pool. His family home seemed more like the dwelling of a movie star than a mob boss. His reclusive life was more bizarre when he openly started an affair with his housekeeper and house cleaner Gloria and entertained his capos while sporting silk or velvet dressing gowns and slippers.

Castellano in the '80s

In 1980, Castellano once again ordered a hit on a man who had abused his daughter. As a family-oriented person, he refused to allow the former hitman and hijacker Frank Amato to live after discovering that he had married Castellano's daughter Connie and immediately began physically abusing her. He called on his trusted friend Roy DeMeo to conduct the hit, and Amato was killed, dismembered, and disposed of at sea in traditional Mafia style; he was sent to sleep with the fishes.

While Castellano resided in his mansion and dispensed orders from behind his front door, the troops were becoming increasingly disgruntled with his methods. He may have answered to the title "Boss of Bosses." Still, John Gotti, a former associate of the passed-over underboss Dellacroce, was planning to expand into the narcotics trade and go against Castellanos's strict directive to leave the industry alone. He was in talks with Roy DeMeo to form links with other families and become part of their drug empire. Although Castellano was becoming increasingly reclusive and greedy, he still had some loyal family members. When word of the Gotti/DeMeo defection reached him, he decided to do something about it.

Castellano was aware of the lack of respect some of his family members had for him, and he sent a message by taking out a contract on his formerly loyal hitman Roy De Meo. Word reached Gotti that a contract had been taken out on his friend but by Castellano because he wanted to disband the DeMeo crew of assassins and form a more businesslike family reputation. Castellano found it hard to find a man to take on the contract as they feared the retribution they would face from the rest of the crew, but eventually, John Gotti stepped forward and accepted the job of killing his friend and partner.

He employed two members of DeMeo's crew to make the killing. Joseph Testa and Anthony Senter arranged a meeting with DeMeo at Testa's home, supposedly to discuss critical issues relating to the family. Reportedly, Testa and Senter shot and killed DeMeo and shoved him in the boot of his car, where he was found ten days later. Some stories of the hit also place hitman Richard Kuklinski at the scene, but the truth will probably never be revealed.

In the aftermath of DeMeo's death, it was revealed that he had been under immense pressure from the FBI to rat on his associates in the Gambino family. He had become paranoid from 1982 until he died in 1983 and would rarely leave the house without a firearm. The rest of the family could sense that changes were on the horizon, with John Gotti, Gene Gotti, and Frank DeCicco all plotting to take charge. One of the main supporters of John Gotti, named Angelo Ruggiero, and Gene Gotti was arrested on charges of dealing in heroin based on tapes the FBI had installed in the house of Ruggiero.

Castellano was incensed and demanded to hear the tapes, but Ruggiero refused to hand them over. By then, Castellano knew his grip on the family was under threat, and he also faced a barrage of charges from the FBI. Between March 1984 and November 1985, he was indicted for several crimes and had to pay over $5 million in bail. The charges included the murders of DeMeo and Eppolito and racketeering, including extortion and narcotics trafficking.

While the family reeled from the charges, a major milestone occurred when popular underboss Dellacroce passed away in December 1985. A lavish wake was held in his honor, and the whole Gambino family attended, with one major exception: Paul Castellano. His failure to attend was the ultimate insult to the Dellacroce family, and they were left in shock at his lack of respect. He further angered loyal members of the family by appointing his bodyguard as the new underboss to replace Dellacroce.

Tommy Billotti was a violent, uncultured loan shark, who possessed none of the skills required by an underboss and lacked the finesse required to deal with other families. The move was seen as an indication that Castellano was targeting the Gotti faction of the family and would try to break them up. It was a well-known fact that Castellano and Bilotti regularly ate breakfast together at a local diner, and it was decided the hit would take place there. Meanwhile, Sammy the bull Gravano told Gotti he had a meeting arranged with Castellano and a couple of other main members of the family at Sparks Steak House on the 16th of December in the early evening.

The Assassination of Castellano

Gotti assembled a crew and placed three hitmen at the entrance of the restaurant, and a another three were positioned further down the street. Gotti was waiting to view the kill in a vehicle across from the steak house. Castellano arrived for the meeting at 5.25 pm, and the primary shooters ran up to him and shot him in the head.

Bilotti was killed as he climbed from the driver's seat and attempted to flee from the scene of the murder. Gotti calmly exited the vehicle he was seated in and came over to view the bodies. He shook the hand of the shooter, John Carneglia, who had shot Castellano in the head.

The Aftermath

The DeMeo crew shooters were arrested and sent to prison for life while the Mafia Commission Trial was in progress. Eleven of the top Mafia bosses were on trial for racketeering and other mob-related crimes. The intention of the FBI and US Attorney Rudi Giuliani was to wipe out the five families and strike at them using their involvement in the Mafia Commission as a reason to prosecute them and send them to prison for the rest of their lives. Eight of the defendants were sentenced; seven received sentences of a hundred years and a hefty fine, while a capo from the Bonanno family served twelve years of his forty-year sentence before being released in 1998. The other mobsters are all dead; they died behind bars at various medical centers within the federal system.

It was all change in the Gambino family. Castellano was refused a Catholic public funeral by order of the Archdiocese of New York because of the nature of his position. He deemed it would indicate the church condones Mafia activities and would, at worst, appear apathetic to the organization. Instead of a public funeral, Castellano was buried in haste in a quiet and unassuming service in a nonsectarian cemetery with minimum mourners attending. A spokesperson for the FBI revealed they were unaware of the event and who had attended. Although some members of the family appeared at the cemetery, there was one noticeable absentee, John Gotti.

CHAPTER 8:
The Gotti Era

J ohn Gotti was the Dapper Don, the Teflon Mobster, and the man who finally brought mob life into the public domain. His whole persona screamed flash gangster, and unlike some of his former bosses, he played the role of the Godfather in the public eye. His name became synonymous with the Mafia and a metaphor for organized crime. He flaunted his power and claimed to be the emperor of the Cosa Nostra, rather than taking a more subdued role in the Gambino family. Don't forget the Mafia Commission Trial was the first time a lot of the public had heard about the extent of the Mafia's business, and the term Cosa Nostra was used. When Gotti was elevated to the boss of the Gambino family, it had twenty-three active crews, over three hundred made men, and over two thousand associates. The family was amassing a fortune with their rackets and legitimate organizations, grossing over half a billion dollars annually. Gotti was paid over ten million dollars per year as part of his income as the head of the family. He declared just a hundred thousand dollars as his income from his legitimate business interests as a plumbing salesperson and garment company employer.

The Early Years

Like many of his predecessors, Gotti came from a lowly background in the Bronx. He was the fifth child of thirteen born to immigrant parents, John and Francis Gotti, who scraped a living in the East New York section. His father was a day laborer, and while his mother took any job, she could only just feed her children. The Gotti's often had to move home regularly because they couldn't pay the rent, and a moonlight flit was the only way they could make ends meet.

Gotti spent his early life running errands for mobsters and local gangsters who worked for Carmine Fatico, a capo who worked for the Gambino family in the 1950s and recognized that young John Gotti had promise. He introduced the teenager to Aniello Dellacroce, who would then take on the role of mentor to the future crime boss. When he reached the age of sixteen, Gotti left school and formed his own crew, called the Fulton-Rockaway Boys, where he met a future Gambino gangster named Angelo Ruggerio.

The crew participated in plenty of petty crimes, like car theft and housebreaking, and engaged in plenty of street fights as they honed their skills as gangsters. They avoided any major crimes for over ten years, but inevitably, the law soon became more interested in Gotti and his gang. John, his brother Gene, and Ruggerio were all arrested for their part in hijacking a truck and stealing cargo from JFK airport. They had been caught red-handed, and all three pled guilty to ensure they received the minimum sentence possible. Gotti served three years and was a much more seasoned gangster when he emerged from behind bars.

Fatico recognized his increase in experience and skills and made Gotti the head of illegal gambling in the area and made him a captain of the family. Although he ran the operation well in 1974, Gotti displayed his future trademark love for the public eye when he was assigned to commit his first murder. In May 1973, Gotti was tasked with the removal of a rival associate who had killed a member of the Gambino family at a bar on Staten Island. The hit was a disaster and led to the killing taking place in full public view, which led to the identification of Gotti by an eyewitness. He was arrested and charged with manslaughter and given a four-year sentence.

Gotti's Family Life

John married Victoria, and they lived in a modest home with their five children, unlike some of the former mob bosses. He may have attracted the public's and the media's attention, but he kept his family life secret. He did have the attention turned to his private life when his twelve-year-old son was killed in a road traffic accident by a local neighbor named John Favara. The family ostensibly went on holiday to Florida to grieve for their loss four months later when Favara went missing. Witnesses reported they saw him being clubbed over the head and shoved in a truck. He was never seen again, and Gotti denied knowing anything about the incident.

Gotti Facts

Gotti became the media don and was a well-known figure on the streets of New York. Here are facts that sum up the character of the Dapper Don, who courted public attention:

- He was so aware of his public persona and his natty dress sense that he had an extra suit on hand during his trial in 1992 so he could change at lunch.

- He had been arrested five times when he celebrated his twenty-first birthday.

- After the accident involving Favara and his son, Gotti's wife attacked the driver with a metal baseball bat.

- Frank Sinatra was scheduled to have dinner with Gotti but pretended to be unwell to get out of the appointment. Gotti sent a heavy to threaten him and make sure he knew Gotti wasn't pleased.

- During the mid-eighties, he avoided being found guilty in three separate trials leading to his nickname, the Teflon Don.

- Gotti loved to gamble and regularly spent $30,000 a night in casinos; one night, he lost over $50,000 in a single dice game.

- Castellano supporters attempted to blow up Gotti following his assassination of the Gambino boss, but they failed and blew up his friend and underboss Frank DeCicco.

- When he was fourteen, he attempted to steal a cement mixer but was left with a permanent limp when a heavy piece of machinery fell on his leg.

- The Fulton – Rockaway Boys were named after Gotti's favorite street in the neighborhood, Rockaway Avenue.

- Ever the gambler, after his arrest in 1990, Gotti offered odds of 3-1 to police officers that he would be found innocent.

- During his trials, there were huge crowds of people outside of the courthouse.

- Gotti's son was quoted as saying there was nothing he didn't like about his life. It was 24/7, and even his wife and kids played second fiddle to the streets.

The Trial of John Gotti

Of course, it couldn't last, and the law eventually caught up with the flamboyant mob boss. The FBI had installed surveillance equipment in an apartment above a social club the mob boss loved to visit. This was the downside to Gotti's public figure status; everybody knew where he was, and he made no secret of his favored social venues. In 1990, they recorded conversations between Sammy the bull Gravano, Gotti, and a family member called Frank Locasio.

Gotti was arrested in December 1990 and must have been confident he would once again evade prison. He hadn't reckoned on the testimonies of certain members of the Gambino family emerging and eventually leading to his being found guilty. Most important was the deal made with Gravano, who flipped on his boss to receive a lighter sentence. When Gotti was indicted in 1985 by the Mafia Commission Trial, he was considered a low-rate hoodlum, who was a minor member of the Gambino hierarchy, but that changed when Castellano and Bilotti were killed. It became common knowledge that Gotti was behind the killing.

Since he took his place as the new boss, Gotti had been mocking law enforcement with his blatant celebrity status. He flaunted his position and made a mockery of the law, and the federal prosecutors needed to prove a point. The prosecution was weakened when Bruce Cutler, Gotti's combative lawyer, argued that tapes of Gotti plotting a hit could be misinterpreted and that his client was trying to bust up crews in the family rather than organize a hit on a member of the Westies crime group. His 1990 trial ended with yet another not-guilty verdict for the Teflon don.

In December of 1990, the US Attorney immediately charged Gotti with a further set of charges, including tax evasion and other multiple felonies. This time, the stage was set for success when the federal prosecutors managed to remove Gotti's lawyer from the trial. They also kept the identity of the judge and jury anonymous and in police protection throughout the trial to avoid tampering from members of the Gambino family. Would this be the trial that finally put Gotti in prison and ended his reign in the Gambino family?

The prosecution had learned from their past mistakes and spoke directly to the jury. They addressed the fact that the main witness for the prosecution was an admitted murderer, but they told the jury that made his evidence more compelling rather than "a rat" who was trying to get a lighter sentence. They heard multiple tapes with the voice of Gotti speaking about murders and other crimes, and he could be heard clearly stating, "Anyone who doesn't agree with us, we kill him." The evidence continued to mount against Gotti, and the only defense witness was his tax lawyer, who had told the mobster not to file tax returns while under formal accusation. The judge ruled out the other five defense witnesses as inappropriate for legal reasons, and this angered the formerly confident mob boss. He lost his cool, openly arguing with the judge and facing the threat of contempt and removal from the courtroom.

Defense attorney Krieger argued the case was built on the lies of a proven murderer, but the prosecutor replied that Gravano was the stuff of nightmares for the mob boss, and that is why they ranted and raved about him. As the jury retired, the mood in the court was hopeful that a conviction would be imminent. They didn't have to wait long; thirteen hours later, the jury found Gotti and his associate Locasio guilty of all charges, and two months later, they were sentenced to life without parole. Meanwhile, Gravano was continuing to spill the beans on the organization. Under the new rules of seizure, the FBI continued to confiscate the ill-gotten gains amassed by the crime family.

Sammy Gravano didn't walk away from his crimes Scot-free. He was sentenced to five years for racketeering charges and released early in 1994 to join the witness protection scheme in Arizona. However, the life of crime called once more, and Sammy couldn't ignore the call. He returned to mob life by organizing an ecstasy trafficking ring with members of his blood family, who were arrested alongside him and forty others in 2000. He served seventeen years of his twenty-year sentence, obtaining his release in 2017. He now enjoys moderate celebrity status with his podcast called "Our Thing," where he continues to tell his story.

The Reign of Junior

In 1992, with Gotti in prison for the rest of his life in solitary, he played his last card for the Gambino family by appointing his son John as the next boss of the Gambinos. The other crime families were incensed by his decision and believed the media interest in such a move would be the downfall of the organization. Their fears proved to be well based, and the spotlight shone on Gotti Jr. when the FBI arrested him and thirty-seven other members of the family for racketeering. The family imploded as they pled guilty en masse to avoid testifying and receive reduced sentences. Gotti Jr. was sent to prison, where he remained for months before his supporters rallied the money to cover his bail.

Gotti Sr. wasn't happy, and he ranted and raved to his daughter that John Jr. was an imbecile and that he was guilty of leaving evidence where investigators could find it. Prosecutors used these tapes to show the involvement of Gotti Jr. in the mob family and argued he shouldn't be given bail. The family was in disarray, and bedlam ensued when the media reported that Jr. would consider a plea bargain even though his father was against the plan. The government applied more pressure by freezing his assets and made it impossible for the family to pay its bills or continue to operate.

At one point, the frustrated defendant asked the judge to send him back to prison to save money.

As the years passed, the pressure mounted until John Jr. decided he would plead guilty to his charges, hoping he could serve his time and emerge from prison to spend the rest of his life with his young wife and family. He had spent years unable to provide them with an income, and he decided he owed it to his family, not the Gambino family, to sort out his priorities and get his house in order. He pleaded guilty to six charges, including extortion and loansharking, and received a sentence of six and a half years of incarceration. The government continued to forfeit properties and money that had become part of the Gambino family fortune through criminal activities, and the organization was devastated by the losses they faced.

John Gotti Sr. was facing his own personal demons, and in 1998, he was operated on because of neck and head cancer. The operation resulted in his life being extended until 2002, when he died in a prison facility in Springfield, Missouri. His funeral was conducted just like his life- big, bold, and ostentatious. A cavalcade of twenty-two black limousines led the procession. They were followed by nineteen black cars carrying flowers and hundreds of vehicles belonging to mourners. He was laid to rest beside the grave of his son Frank in St. Johns Cemetery, a popular resting place for many mob members.

As the funeral procession slowly made its way through the streets, many weeping mourners could be heard shouting, "We love you, John," as the larger-than-life funeral tributes poured in. Even today, you can see footage of the funeral and tributes to Gotti with stark warnings that, if you post any negative comments, there will be consequences.

What Happened to John Gotti Jr.?

While he was still incarcerated, Junior was charged with further racketeering indictments and was a suspect in the plot to kidnap a member of the Guardian Angels. They had badmouthed Gotti Sr. on the radio. The next two years were filled with four trials on the charges, with Junior sticking to his story that he gave up his Mafia connections after his conviction in 1999. Further allegations and charges were brought in 2008, and Gotti was seen in the dock.

A former Gambino family member turned state witness and gave evidence against Gotti in court, which led to a public slanging match between the mob traitor, John Alite, and Gotti Jr., with the latter mouthing the words, "I'll kill you," at his former associate. The press had a field day with the chaos surrounding the proceedings. Eventually, in December 2009, the twelve jury members reported they had failed to reach a decision on the charges, and a mistrial was declared by the judge.

After the trial, several members of the jury spoke to the press and declared the entire process was ridiculous and made a mockery of the law. To be honest, the infighting and testimonies of former mob members couldn't be relied on, and the whole process had become shambolic. The government decided enough was enough, and pursuing another trial against Gotti would be pointless.

Gotti Jr. then claimed to have left the mob and cut all ties with the Gambino family. He spent the years following his release quietly raising his six kids and being a model husband to his wife, Kimberley. Still, he did show similarities to his father's persona when he authored his book, *Shadow of My Father*, a memoir of his time in the mob, which he then allowed to be turned into a film in 2018.

Shadow of My Father Was Released as a Film Called *Gotti*

In the film, John Travolta played John Sr., while his real-life wife played Gotti's wife, Victoria. Stacy Keach played the role of Dellacroce, with William DeMeo portraying Sammy Gravano. The soundtrack was Blondie, and the movie received seven nominations in categories that weren't particularly flattering. It was hailed as the worst movie of the year with the worst actor and actress awards for Travolta and Preston and a nomination for a Razzie.

Junior has actively voiced his dislike of the film and has said it didn't do justice to his story, but he did participate in a promotional tour for the movie. He has also filled his social media with images of him with the film's two stars and seems to revel in the attention the movie brought him. The movie may have been a disaster, but it did mean the name of John Jr. was once again catapulted into the public eye.

CHAPTER 9:
Gotti, Cefalu, and Cali

Peter Gotti had been part of the Gambino family for as long as anyone could remember, but he never displayed the qualities required for the position of a boss; with his brother just days from his death and Junior in prison, he stepped up and took the reins in 2002. His kind demeanor and lack of psychopathic tendencies gave him the unenviable nickname of the "Dumbest Don Ever." To be fair to Peter, he was elevated through the ranks based solely on his name and would never have reached public attention if he hadn't been a Gotti.

In 2002, weeks after formally accepting the role as boss of the family, Peter was indicted for racketeering. During his trial, the prosecutor dropped a bombshell that would change his life and bring his family nothing but grief. He had been happily married for over forty years to his wife, Catherine, and they had one child. In court, the prosecutor revealed he had been involved in a love affair with a woman twenty years his junior, Marjorie Alexander. Later, she would go public with a declaration of her love for the mobster and state she was proud of their love and would stand by her man.

The mob culture included mistresses and long-time girlfriends, but the golden rule remained that they were kept in the background and never embarrassed their families. In one way, they are classed as an essential accouterment in mob culture, and most mobsters had affairs, but, in this case, Gotti's wife wasn't impressed when Alexander wrote to the judge about Peter and his character. She berated her husband for his lack of finesse and told the press he deserved everything he got. Gotti broke off all communication with Alexander and told the press she should have kept quiet during the trial. Alexander was found in a motel room in Long Island the following year with a plastic bag over her head and several suicide notes at the scene. Her death was ruled a suicide, and it seems unlikely the Gambino family had anything to do with the death.

Gotti was sentenced to nine years and four months for his crimes, including attempted extortion of the screen actor Steven Seagal. As he served his time, he faced further charges relating to other charges, including plotting to eradicate the mob informant Sammy the bull Gravano. He was sentenced to a further twenty-five years in prison despite his lawyers arguing he should be treated leniently because of his ill health. Gotti was blind in one eye, suffering from gout, sciatica, arthritis, and mental health issues, including depression.

He continued to be the titular leader of the family until the accession of Domenico Cefalu in 2011, but he was a broken man after losing his long-time lover and his divorce from his wife. It was common knowledge that Cefalu was more than just an underboss, and he was well-liked and respected by the Sicilian branch of the family. A series of acting bosses and panels of leaders had been responsible for the family business since 2002, and the installation of Cefalu marked a return to the older Mafia ways of running the business, and he was welcomed by all the Cosa Nostra factions.

Peter Gotti died in a medical facility in Butner, North Carolina, of natural causes, and with his death, the Gotti name faded from the headlines and marked the end of an era that some would say had expired in 2002. His son Peter Gotti Jr. appeared briefly in the media when he was arrested for drug charges in 2016 and was refused a deal with the DA despite it being his first conviction. The twenty-three-year-old was given a sentence of twenty years, which he claims was based solely on his surname.

Domenico Cefalu

Some reports state Cefalu took official control of the Gambino family in 2021, but it seems unlikely the firm could have grown and flourished as it has without a strong leader. Cefalu is an old-time mobster, who believes in getting the job done without attracting the attention of the law or the media. He reportedly ran the family since 2011 without registering on the radar of either organization and has been the steadying hand on the tiller of the Gambino ship.

Early Years of Cefalu

Cefalu was born in 1947 and was the son of an Italian mother before moving to the US and becoming part of the Gambino family. He was part of a successful gang that concentrated on shipping heroin and smuggling other narcotics. He served alongside his uncle and cousin until they were caught in 1982 and served six years in prison for his involvement. When he emerged from prison, his silence when questioned by the law was rewarded when John Gotti, the serving boss, awarded him with the title of a made man. He became part of the notorious Zip crew, headed by respected caporegime Patsy Conte, who operated in the Queens area of New York.

When the law caught up with Conte in 1992, Cefalu was summoned to testify, but after answering a couple of random questions, he refused to testify anymore. He was given an eighteen-month sentence for contempt and sent to prison to serve his time. As Cante's trial progressed, the judge repeatedly called for Cefalu to testify and was met with refusals; Cefalu was steadfast in his loyalty and spent the next six years in and out of prison because he failed to open his mouth.

Cefalu in the 21st Century

The Gambino family continued to evolve, and one man to emerge from the shadows was Jackie D'Amico, who was appointed Street Boss, a number one position following the era of John Gotti and his leadership from behind bars. He was reportedly made boss in 2003, along with Jo Coruzzo and Zeke Squitieri as his main advisors. In 2005, D'Amico appointed Cefalu as underboss, and he was given the job of organizing the Sicilian faction of the family.

Operation Old Bridge

In 2008, the FBI began an operation to collect information through an informant named Joe Vollaro regarding the Gambino family's involvement in drug trafficking and racketeering in New York. Corozzo was tipped off by a family member that the FBI was coming for him, and he fled and went into hiding. Cefalu was indicted for multiple charges relating to the rackets around the construction industry. Cefalu organized an extortion ring to extract funds from the truck companies that hauled dirt away from construction sites.

The name Old Bridge is derived from the historical ties between the Sicilian and New York Mafia. Some members of the Sicilian faction had been "allowed" to relocate to the US to avoid retribution from the Italian mafia, provided they promised never to set foot in Sicily again. The Gambino family had brokered deals on behalf of the Italian emigres and welcomed them into their family. Despite these pledges, some of the exiled Mafia members yearned for their homeland. They returned to Sicily, forming important drug trafficking routes between the homeland and America, known as The Bridge. They were forming lucrative ties and reestablishing the drug routes between the two countries, and the authorities needed to act.

Several members of the Gambino family were amongst the eighty people indicted. When Corozzo decided he couldn't cope with life on the run anymore, he rejoined the family and turned himself in. Of all the American defendants, just two pleaded not guilty; the other sixty entered a guilty plea and served their sentence in prison.

The Gambino members who were given the harshest sentences included:

- Frank Cali, an acting underboss and one of the self-appointed ambassadors to the Sicilian faction, received sixteen months for conspiracy and was released in June 2009.

- Charlie Carneglia was found guilty of four murders and given life imprisonment.

- Domenico Cefalu was given two years for extortion and released in November 2009.

- Jo Corozzo was found guilty of conspiracy and given a sentence of three years and ten months.

- Little Nick Corozzo, a captain of the Gambino family, was sentenced to thirteen years and six months for one count of murder and conspiracy. He was released in March 2020.

- Jackie D'Amico received two years for corruption and was released in November 2009.

- Richard Gotti, the cousin of Junior Gotti, was given eight years for attempted murder and released in 2015.

Cefalu and Cali Take Control

Since his release in 2009, Domenico Cefalu has stayed out of the limelight and kept the Gambino family business running without attracting attention from the law or the media. There are stories about the organization now and then, but its leaders still know the benefits of anonymity. It was believed that, as Cefalu aged, he shared his position with his former protégé Cali and began to hand over the reins completely. However, these plans were shattered when Cali was gunned down in 2019, forcing Cefalu to regain control of the family.

The Death of Frank Cali

When he was gunned down in March 2019, Cali was the first reported New York boss to be assassinated since the death of Paul Castellano in 1985. The circumstances were unusual for a mob hit. When the police reviewed the surveillance tape of the shooting, it showed a pickup truck deliberately hitting Cali's Cadillac and the driver emerging to confront the mobster. Despite using the Cadillac as a shield, the gunman put ten bullets in Cali and left him dead on the sidewalk.

Three days later, the police arrested a young man named Anthony Comello for the murder. One news report stated the reasons behind the killing were "romantic and personal" rather than related to organized crime. When the trial started, Comello's defense attorney told the court the defendant was deeply involved with the QAnon movement that had originated in 2017 and involved false claims made by an individual named Q regarding the far-right conspiracy theories. Comello was convinced he was authorized by President Trump to arrest and detain Cali for his mafia connections.

The defense offered evidence that Comello had attempted to arrest other individuals, including the NY Mayor Bill de Blasio. During his court appearance, Comello had various symbols and quotes from the QAnon movement scrawled on his hand and arms and appeared erratic and confused. Following a mental examination, he was ruled unfit to stand trial, and he was committed to a mental hospital where he remains today.

Who Is in Charge Today?

Most Mafia sources recognize the Gambino family is still the foremost family in New York and is still raking in millions of dollars from their criminal and legitimate activities. Who is in charge? Cefalu or a new boss? Lorenzo Mannino is a name that keeps cropping up when the Gambino family is mentioned, and he is a powerful figure in the family and has been part of the administration team for years. Is he now the boss of the family? And the wonderful part of mob lore is that, unless it benefits the family to release the information, we will never know for sure. Cali would probably be in charge if he hadn't fallen foul of a mental patient, but he did, and things had to change.

Cefalu is now in his seventies, and while it isn't unusual for mob bosses to be that age, he must be ready to step back and retire, but has he given Mannino the official title of the boss? Watch out for him and others stepping up to take charge. Even though the era of flashy dons with pimped-out cars and expensive suits is over. Following the 9/11 attacks, many FBI agents were reassigned to terrorism, away from organized crime, which meant the Cosa Nostra was given a chance to regroup and become more organized. Reduced scrutiny led to the five families and other groups of mobsters reconnecting and forming lucrative ties.

CHAPTER 10:
What Is the Relevance of the Mafia Today?

T he Golden Era of organized crime seems to be an historic event, but is it because we have all accepted that crime will always be part of society and organized crime doesn't affect the man on the street? Do Mafia activities still interest us, and do we know anyone who is involved? In this chapter, we will ask some of the more pertinent questions that arise and then look at more famous people with Mafia ties.

Question 1: Do the Five Families Still Exist?

They are all active but to varying degrees. The death of Carmine Persico in 2019 meant the Colombo family lacked a leader. Despite being imprisoned for life, Persico still ran the family from his cell and maintained a three-man committee to perform his wishes on the outside. The Colombo family knew they would have to conform, but the infighting and deceit meant the family had big decisions to make.

As in the past, the Gambino and Genovese families are prominent families, but this means they are also families under constant scrutiny by the law. The Bonanno and Lucchese families exist, but they operate in the shadows. The rackets are different; online opportunities have provided a more technical way to produce income, while the old rackets continue to bring in income. The main difference between the past and current families is that they fail to make headlines anymore. There are more spectacular and headline-grabbing criminals and gangsters for the press to deal with now.

Question 2: Which Is the Most Successful Family in New York?

If the question had been which family courts the most press attention, the answer would be the Gambino family, but behind the scenes, the Genovese family has continued to grow. They have the most active members, and their boss is an expert at future-proofing their income streams for generations to come. Bellomo, the head of the Genovese family, has been in power since 1990 and is well-respected and well-aware that keeping out of the limelight is the way to succeed. Both families are much smaller than they were in their heyday, but they are adapting to modern methods to secure their future.

Question 3: Which Is the Least Successful Family?

We have touched on the Colombo family and their inner turmoil. Unfortunately, that has been the case since the 1990s, when they suffered their third and most devastating family war. Thirteen people died, and scores of their members were arrested and ultimately jailed. The Colombo family was decimated, and their name was slurred, meaning they failed to replace their lost soldiers, and their ranks were gutted. Today, they have just a handful of captains and crews on the streets of New York that are tolerated because of history.

Question 4: Are There Any Active Families Outside of New York?

The Outfit

Chicago was once the hub of Mafia action, and tales of Al Capone and his bootlegging industry is the stuff of legends. They are known as "the Outfit," and they had a strong leader in Tony Accardo, who served until he died in 1992. The most recent blow to the Outfit came when the FBI organized a campaign dubbed the Family Secrets Operation to target the members of the Chicago operation. In 1998, the Calabrese family imploded, and several members snitched on their leaders and gave the FBI information about a range of crimes dating back as far as the 1970s. Three of their leaders were sentenced to life in prison, and eight of their top men were incarcerated. While defectors and snitches aren't unheard of in Mafia circles, the testimony of the successful assassin and son of the leader Nick Calabrese sealed the fate of the organization.

They have a leader at the moment, but he is eighty years old and seems to have no obvious successor. Chicago isn't an attractive mob destination anymore, although there is still money to be made from traditional racketeering options, like gambling, extortion, and drug trafficking.

The Bruno Family

Based in Philadelphia, this family was named after their most famous don, Angelo Bruno. He reigned in Philly for the majority of the '60s and '70s and was a wise leader who brought prosperity and peace to the organization. Unfortunately, this changed in March 1980, when Angelo was shot in the back of the head as he sat in his car outside his home. He was succeeded by don Testa, who was killed by his own underboss when one of his men detonated a bomb underneath his car just a year later.

The next boss of the Bruno family was a certified lunatic, named Nicky Scarfo, who started his reign by mindlessly killing over a dozen people for no reason. His troops turned on him and testified against the unpopular boss in the mid-1980s, leading to a sentence of fifty-five years, fourteen years, and life for three separate offenses. He died in jail in 2017 of natural causes. In the 1990s, there was a huge power struggle in the Bruno ranks that eventually led to a standoff between a young Turk and an old-school mafia type. John Stanfa, the young Turk, was eventually beaten by the veteran known as Skinny Joey Merlino.

He may not have the personality and natural leadership qualities that some other bosses displayed, but he has brought a sense of unity to the family. Although he is serving a prison sentence, he still runs the family with the help of his loyal crew. His trusted team runs the business while he is away and is loyal to their boss, for now, anyway.

Patriarca Family

In Mafia and organized crime circles, Boston has always been different from the organizations running in New York and Chicago. The Boston scene has strong ties with Ireland rather than Italy. The most prominent family is the Patriarca family, which is based in Rhode Island and has been around for about a century. Their most successful years were under the leadership of Raymond Patriarca Sr., who kept the organization balanced and successful for decades before his death in 1984.

Following his death, his son Raymond took over the family and proved to be a dreadful boss with none of his father's qualities. He retired, and there followed a period of unrest in the family with members turning state evidence and ratting out their crew.

Balance was restored in 2009 when a prominent businessperson and well-respected name in New England took control. Peter Limone was a safe hand on the tiller for the family, and they regained their former territories. He shares the leadership with a seasoned gangster, called DiNunzio, and has shifted the business to Providence. They have around forty men in the organization and function beneath the radar despite the opposition from local media. Other mafia families are still operating, but these are the main ones.

Question 6: What Is the Main Reason for the Demise of the Mafia?

The code of omerta was once the most powerful code of the Mafia. No matter what, the member knew they wouldn't betray their fellow Mafioso even under the threat of death. Joe Valachi spectacularly broke that code when he became the first mobster to acknowledge and confirm the existence of the Cosa Nostra. He didn't just tell the world about the organization. He described all their most treasured secrets and rituals.

Once this betrayal happened, the Mafia lost its most powerful tool. The law enforcement agencies knew it was possible to break the code of silence, and the floodgates were open. Although the code of omerta survived a few decades longer, it was damaged, but in 1991, the dam broke when a Gambino family underboss, Sammy Gravano, turned state witness to help send his boss John Gotti to prison. Despite admitting to his part in nineteen murders, Sammy "the bull" Gravano received a diminished prison sentence for his cooperation.

Question 7: Can There Ever Be a Revival of the Mafia?

The answer must be NO. They will never regain the status they had in the heady days of Luciano and Gambino. They couldn't exist in the fast-moving world in which we find ourselves today. Yes, there are families still on the streets of America, but they are smaller operations and fail to mirror that bond the first five families and their Mafia counterparts formed.

Question 8: What Rackets Are Outdated Now?

Extortion. The others are still a source of income; gambling, and vice, along with narcotics, always will be around, but extortion and protection are definitely old school. Modern technology means the gangs still trying to intimidate people have more chance of being caught with modern surveillance improvements. There is less chance of getting away with murder in modern times, and today's Mafia rarely resorts to old-time hits and assassinations.

Question 9: What Rackets Are Still Profitable?

Loan sharking is still the main base of most Mafia finances. People always need money, and gangsters have a large supply. They charge extortionate interest rates, but for some people, they are the only option. Other rackets are more likely to attract the law, but desperate people stay quiet because the Mafia offer a service they need, no matter the consequences.

Question 10: Does Anyone Want to Join the Mafia Today?

Yes, because young men still recognize the kudos of being a gangster, and despite the grim reality of life, they still seek to be the next Godfather. The promise of a quick buck and the status they can have far outweighs the probability of prison or early death. Can you get rich and powerful? Yes, but it comes at a price.

Question 11: Does the Mafia Have Any Influence in Politics?

The simple answer is a resounding NO. Thank goodness those days are gone when mob bosses rubbed shoulders with politicians, and stories that the CIA recruited Mafia hitmen to take out Castro and JFK are a thing of the past.

Question 12: Does the Structure Created by Lucky Luciano Still Work?

Yes. Most families have the same structures in place with a boss and underbosses and the capo level below them. There are fewer associates, and the number of made men has gone down, but they are in place.

Famous People and Their Mob Ties

The Mafia may have lost its connections to the political world, but they still court certain celebrities. Here are a couple of famous people who were attracted by the danger, the kudos, and the sheer thrill of mixing with the Mafia.

Elizabeth Hurley Was Associated with the Colombo Family

This English actress may be intrinsically linked to Hugh Grant, but she dallied with a Colombo family enforcer, Donnie Shacks, for a while even though he was thrown in jail for his part in a racket in New York. The odd couple (she was thirty-five, and he was sixty-seven) was spotted canoodling in a restaurant in Beverly Hills. Was this romance or just a shrewd move on Hurley's part to finance a movie? Who knows?

Wayne Newton Connected to the Gambino Family

This highly successful crooner was reportedly associated with the mob after he confessed to having several friends in the family. He claimed these friendships arose through his performances in Vegas and were totally innocent. He later sued NBC over an article claiming he was a frontman for the family and won undisclosed damages.

James Caan Connected to the Columbo Family

When you look at the cast of the *Godfather* movie, you may be tempted to think Pacino or Brando may have mob ties. Al Pacino and the mob? Maybe but you'd be wrong. James Caan has repeatedly and very publicly shown his support for the Colombo family and even offered to stand bail for Andy Mush, the street boss of the family, when he was arrested in 2009.

The relationship has been in place since the early seventies, and there are rumors that, when he was on the set of the *Godfather*, Caan took offense at the actor Joe Pesci regarding a hotel bill and used his mob connections to get someone to rough him up to show his displeasure. While the other evidence may be circumstantial, there is a damning part to this story. The Mush is the ACTUAL Godfather to Caan's son Scott.

Steven Seagal Is Associated with the Gambino Family

Seagal isn't the best martial arts actor in the business, but he did have some pretty dangerous links with the mob, even if he didn't realize it at the time. His business partner Julius Nasso was embroiled with the Gambino family and failed to tell his cash cow client. When Seagal became spiritually enlightened and decided to pursue other ways to make money, the mob reacted badly. His movies may be rubbish, but they made the Gambino family a lot of cash. They tried to force the actor to return to his violent movie genre, and this led to him taking the stand against Peter Gotti and sending him and some other gangsters to prison.

Unfortunately for the rest of us, it didn't take long for Seagal to realize he didn't have another option for making money, and the crappy violent films continued to get made.

Marilyn Monroe and Joe DiMaggio Associated with the Gambino Family

The power couple of the fifties and early sixties, these two regularly made headlines regarding their turbulent relationship and their involvement with President JFK and mob ties. Marilyn reportedly spent her last night in the company of gangster Sam Giancana, with the gangster pressuring her to keep her affair with Kennedy secret.

Joe DiMaggio also had ties with the Gambino family through his family, and some conspiracy theories tied him to the death of JFK. Reports suggest he used his mob connections to kill the President, believing he was the reason his beloved Marilyn was dead.

Frank Sinatra Associated with Them All

The poster boy of the link between the Mafia and celebrities, Ol' Blue Eyes, was a close friend of many nefarious gangsters and was regularly seen in their company. Sinatra's uncle was heavily involved with the Cosa Nostra, and Frank loved to trade on his notoriety.

Donald Trump Is Associated with the Genovese Family

Way before the political era, Trump was heavily involved in real estate and especially successful in developing casinos in Atlantic City. Reports of his using mob ties to help him buy land cheap and get around labor laws were rife. He was reportedly seen having sit-downs with the big boss of the Genovese family Tony Salerno to make sure his empire would continue to thrive when he moved his attention to New York.

CONCLUSION

Will the Mafia always be part of our lives, or will it fade away into the annals of history? Who knows, maybe at the time of the highwaymen, some people believed they would be around forever. What is patently obvious is that human nature will always contain a desire to make money quickly and without consequences. Organized crime is littered with violent deaths, disappearances, and gruesome tales of torture, but this life still appeals to some young men, as they believe the glamor and riches are worth the risk of death or imprisonment. Reality television and podcasts are also attracting former gangsters and mob members and offering them a way to regain their former notoriety and status. Should we be encouraging this? Is it immoral for former criminals to be famous for their activities? Again, human nature means we are often fascinated by the lives of people who have taken a different path from our own.

Mafia life is filled with tall tales, huge personalities, and tales of activities that are so far-fetched that they seem fictional. Of course, we know they are real, but because most of us won't need to deal with the fallout, we enjoy the stories before returning to our ordinary lives. For some, the effects of the Mafia and the mob have been devastating, so we must remember that fact.

REFERENCES

"20 Questions about the Mafia | Mafia Hitters." Mafiahitters.com, mafiahitters.com/20-questions-about-the-mafia/.

"Active Mafia Families in the United States (2021) | Mafia Hitters." Mafiahitters.com, mafiahitters.com/active-mafia-families-in-the-united-states/.

Bertram, Colin. "The Life and Death of John Gotti." Biography, 21 June 2019, www.biography.com/news/john-Gotti-ae-documentary-Gotti-godfather-son.

Crypto Wallet Portfolio – Just Another WordPress Site. www.loginstep.co/.

Cutler, Nick. "30 Interesting and Bizarre Facts about Carlo Gambino." Tons of Facts, 8 Dec. 2018, tonsoffacts.com/30-interesting-and-bizarre-facts-about-Carlo-Gambino/.

---. "30 Terrifying and Bizarre Facts about Albert Anastasia." Tons of Facts, 29 Nov. 2018, tonsoffacts.com/30-terrifying-and-bizarre-facts-about-Albert-Anastasia/.

https://www.facebook.com/AmericanMafiaHistory. "Ignazio Lupo - Implicated in the Early 1900'S Barrel Murders - American Mafia History." American Mafia History, 27 Apr. 2014, americanmafiahistory.com/ignazio-Lupo/.

https://www.facebook.com/StrengthBySonny. "La Cosa Nostra: The 10 Laws of the Sicilian Mafia (and How They Apply to You) • Strength by Sonny." Strength by Sonny, 2 Sept. 2014, strengthbysonny.com/2014/09/02/la-Cosa-nostra/.

"Is Domenico Cefalù Still the Boss of the Gambino Crime Family?" About the Mafia, 22 Jan. 2020, aboutthemafia.com/is-Domenico-Cefalu-still-the-boss-of-the-gambino-crime-family/.

ISIS. "The Gotham Center for New York City History." The Gotham Center for New York City History, 17 Oct. 2019, www.gothamcenter.org/blog/material-politics-of-new-york-from-the-mafias-concrete-club-to-isis.

Joe Aiello - the American Mafia. 28 Mar. 2020, www.onewal.com/joe-aiello/.

"John Gotti Trial: 1992 | Encyclopedia.com." Www.encyclopedia.com, www.encyclopedia.com/law/law-magazines/john-Gotti-trial-1992.

Kuroski, John. "Mobster Albert Anastasia Made a Fortune in Murder — and Then Lost at His Own Game." All That's Interesting, 20 Feb. 2018, allthatsinteresting.com/albert-anastasia.

Mead, Wendy. "The Truth about Crime Boss Paul Castellano." Grunge.com, 6 May 2021, www.grunge.com/402776/the-truth-about-crime-boss-paul-castellano/.

Mir, Michele "Big Mike," and a: Genovese Crime Family Consigliere-The Members Only Podcast says. "Vincent "the Executioner" Mangano: The Original Gambino Crime Family Boss | the Members Only Podcast." Membersonlypodcast.com, 8 Jan. 2022, membersonlypodcast.com/vincent-mangano-the-original-gambino-crime-family-boss/.

"Salvatore "Toto" D'Aquila - First Boss of the Gambino Family." American Mafia History, 24 Mar. 2014, americanmafiahistory.com/salvatore-toto-daquila/.

"Stefano "The Undertaker" Magaddino." American Mafia History, 1 June 2020, americanmafiahistory.com/stefano-the-undertaker-magaddino/.

Sutton, J. "The Italian Mafia & the Formation of Cosa Nostra." Criminal Behaviours, 30 Jan. 2022, www.criminalbehaviours.com/post/the-Italian-mafia-the-formation-of-cosa-nostra.

"The Black Hand - GangRule." Gangrule.com, 2019, www.gangrule.com/gangs/the-black-hand.

"The Five Families." The New York Mafia, thenewyorkmafia.com/five-families-new-york-mafia/.

"The List of Murder Inc Hitmen." Mafiahitters.com, mafiahitters.com/who-were-the-murder-inc-shooters/.

"The Little King of Garbage: New York Mobster Vincent Squillante." Gangsters Inc. - Www.gangstersinc.org, 3 Oct. 2021, gangstersinc.org/blog/the-little-king-of-garbage-new-york-mobster-vincent-squillante.

"The Real Truth behind Apalachin & the Top Hoodlum Program - the NCS." National Crime Syndicate, 16 Apr. 2020, www.nationalcrimesyndicate.com/the-real-truth-behind-apalachin-the-top-hoodlum-program/.

"Who Was Carlo Gambino? Everything You Need to Know." Www.thefamouspeople.com, www.thefamouspeople.com/profiles/carlo-gambino-8923.php.

"Who Was Paul Castellano? Everything You Need to Know." Www.thefamouspeople.com, www.thefamouspeople.com/profiles/paul-castellano-3396.php.

Wil Fulton. "11 Celebrities You Didn't Know Had Ties to the Mafia." Thrillist, Thrillist, 31 July 2015, www.thrillist.com/culture/famous-people-connected-to-the-mob-what-celebrities-are-in-the-mafia-frank-sinatra-mob-ties.

Printed in Great Britain
by Amazon

24458360R00066